MICHAEL'S CLARION CALL

MICHAEL'S CLARION CALL

*Messages from the Archangel for
Creating Heaven on Earth*

Mary Soliel

TWELVE
TWELVE
PUBLISHING
Boulder, Colorado

Michael's Clarion Call

Messages from the Archangel for Creating Heaven on Earth

Twelve Twelve Publishing, LLC, books may be ordered through booksellers or Amazon.com.

Twelve Twelve Publishing, LLC
P.O. Box 822
Louisville, CO 80027 U.S.A.
www.twelvetwelvepublishing.com
alighthouse@mac.com

Logo Design: Lisa Kubik

Because of the dynamic nature of the Internet, any Web addresses or links contained in this book may have changed since publication and may no longer be valid.

ISBN: 978-0-9890169-8-8

This book
is dedicated to
you,
the reader,
who is achieving greater heights
than humankind has ever
known.

Contents

Acknowledgments

My heart is most ever grateful to Archangel Michael for gracing me with the supreme honor of being a channel for his beautiful messages which have created such joy and anticipation in my heart, and oftentimes with a river of tears of gratitude. And to all my angels and guides, who have so lovingly guided me every step of the way to this very moment, I love and appreciate you all.

I extend my deep thanks to those souls who have greatly supported me on the incredible journey of creating this book: Most especially, to my dear, beloved children, Scott and Karen, whose loving and beautiful ways of being have served as my best preview of what our glorious new world will be like. To my parents, for their unconditional love. To Clare Gippo, for her relentless belief in me and who first taught me that we all need to just "be love." To Julie Libcke, my friend of many lifetimes who is with me no matter our physical distance. To Cindy Winston, for her golden, loving support. To author, Sherri Cortland, N.D., who provided invaluable, generous help and advice while previewing this book. To Talia Batini, a beautiful example of pure, loving kindness. To Jeannie Barnes, whose guidance helped me immeasurably. To Ron Guthrie, for his depth of support which was especially treasured when going out on a limb with new information. To Helen Palmer who enthusiastically displays such faith in my work. And to Lisa Kubik, Angelita Loré, Mia Milharycic, Petra Densborn-Moeller, Laura Schamahorn, Jennifer Seeley, Jessica Watson, Maria Weber, Nicola Whitehill and so many others, including those mentioned in my first book, who have been a constant source of inspiration and joy in my life, and I thank you all.

Author's Note

Dear Reader,

Thank you for finding your way to this book. Some may not believe that these messages are real and truly received from Archangel Michael. As I experienced powerful signs that validated my new role as a channel for him, and then received various messages over time, I realized that these messages would ring profoundly true and often not resemble anything that has ever been in my own personal thoughts. Michael has presented me with signs and miracles proving again and again that this is, indeed, very real.

When I first learned that I would be a channel of Michael, it took convincing myself that ordinary me was actually worthy of this new role. But those thoughts went away once I actually connected with Michael. He immediately made me feel that he was my friend and I was indeed worthy to receive Heaven-sent messages, *as we all are*. I grew to realize that we all can channel; and we actually do so, often without knowing it.

Eight years prior to my writing of this book, I channeled several messages from Michael, some of which are included here. The concept of time is much debated, and, interestingly, the messages received from Michael so long ago have absolute relevance to what is occurring right now. In reviewing the original messages, it is clear that they were a preview of what was to come for this book, and, in fact, the "Prelude" and "Introduction" were taken directly from these early channels.

In the first chapter, I include personal channels from Michael. I pushed past my comfort zone in order to share the fuller meaning and history of my experience. Even though it may appear at times as if I'm blowing my own horn, I know that I am not more special or important than anyone else. And if and when you choose to channel, you will hear extraordinary things about yourself, as well, because you will learn about who you really are, too.

As always, I discern everything I read and hear, including, and most especially, everything I channel. My greatest intention is that I present the truth. As you read the messages from Michael, if they help you and ring true in your heart, then allow the messages to speak for themselves. Let them mirror the truth in your own lives. By being open to the new way of being that is described within these pages, you will be led to a golden existence.

Please note that this book has not been professionally edited to preserve the authenticity of the messages and conversations without the lesser concern of perfect grammar. Channeling the Heavenly realms is a most natural process, and I receive just as I speak, not perfectly, but with perfect intentions to bring forth wisdom with clarity and truth.

~ Mary Soliel

Prelude

Beloved seekers: You who are reading this book, you who perhaps follow a deep inner knowing that this information is sacred and meaningful even when it does not follow your present belief structures, you are applauded for your courage, faith, and open mind. The open mind is the key, dear ones, to the ever-expanding wealth of knowledge that is bestowed on you. Mary Soliel, my partner in these communications contracted with me to perform this task prior to her incarnation. She was chosen for her desire to seek only the truth. Her path has not been easy; she has held steadfast to her faith even when the messages seemed confusing, frustrating, or plain wrong. This is the message she wants to impart, the message of relentless faith, because she has lived it. I am Archangel Michael.

Introduction

Dear Friends, you have in your hands a volume of messages that can quite literally change your life, if you so desire. You see, there is a spiritual revolution on the rise, and you have the choice to either join the collective souls who are in the midst of seeking love and peace on earth, or those who continue to live in a place of fear. If you choose the former, you will receive the Light of God to aid you in your wondrous endeavors. If the latter choice is made, you will be honored for your chosen path as you exercise your right of free will, and you will continue to live in the same reality.

Let me begin by expressing the wonderful opportunity that lies before you. Can you imagine an earth that thrives on love, not fear; on peace, and not war? This is where your planet is heading. The old ways are not going to work anymore, and the Clarion Call is being sounded as the time of decision making is here. When you join the forces of Light, you hereby reject all lower energies that no longer resonate to your new level of existence. This means that your thoughts and actions, your desires and behaviors, and your friends and acquaintances that no longer mesh with your new level of being, will leave you or at least no longer have prominence in your life. You will be cleansed and refreshed for new and higher opportunities, relationships, and states of being.

Does this all sound like "new age" idle nonsense? You can label it as some may. The fact is this world is changing and you can no longer ignore the signs. Step up and make your choice now. The moment you voice your intent, the world through your eyes will change. If you choose to accept the direction your earth is heading, you will begin to shed the layers of self that no longer serve you. Many of you naturally resist change, but I tell you that you must learn to embrace it with your whole being. You must seek the wisdom and understanding that will allow you to persevere through the discomforts and feelings of insecurity related to the waves of change. There are legions of us in the Heavenly realms who are waiting to serve you. You can call on us at any time. I will tell you again and again that you are not alone and you are dearly loved. You have an immeasurable amount of guidance available, just yours for the asking.

The prophecies of destruction and despair for the earth no longer exist as potential realities. Enough of you, albeit a small percentage of humankind, voiced intent to the Universe to change the prophesied paradigm and create a new earth. Therefore, the earth and its occupants are on a new path and there is much to be celebrated, but there is also much to be healed. The earth body has suffered such pain through the eons of time and she has, especially in recent years, been going through a cycle of great release of the pains inflicted on her. This is the explanation for the strange weather patterns, the increase in earthquakes, storms, and other violent acts of nature. This isn't the end of the earth; it is a releasing and healing for a new beginning! What the earth is going through, you have, are, or will be going through too, on an individual level. You need to release and heal as you move towards your new beginning, as well.

My precious ones, this is a time like no other in your earth's history. The messages in this book are written for those who choose the Light, who no longer want to live in fear, who are tired of the old ways, and who choose to create Heaven on earth. I am Archangel Michael, Master and Protector of the Light.

~ Archangel Michael, January 2002

CHAPTER 1

The First Messages from Archangel Michael

Preparing for a move to a new home can introduce all types of new beginnings, beyond the obvious ones. One mid-November morning in 2009, I was pruning down the heaps of paper in my cluttered office getting ready for my family's move, when I encountered something beyond wonderful, and what would materialize into a most auspicious new beginning: the creation of this very book.

I came across something that I myself had prepared and fully remember preparing, but had not read through in years. The white binder titled, "Archangel Michael: Personal Channelings (the beginning)" profoundly caught my attention. Feeling a strong urge to drop what I was doing, as if directed by unseen forces, I reconnected with the first messages I received from Archangel Michael eight years ago, almost exactly to the day the first message came through.

Reading through the dozens of messages from the Archangel, it was as if I had never read them before. I had forgotten so much and felt confused regarding why I put this binder away. There were absolute gems of information throughout, and I read them with wide-eyed disbelief. The answer suddenly became clear; I was confused because there were some key things that Archangel Michael had described, things that hadn't come true years ago, and so I set the material aside. What I came to find out was that I was meant to reconnect with this information given to me as a preview then, but destined to be shared in the future—which is right now—at this most perfect time.

Michael told me in these messages that I would begin writing a book in three months. Once I found these old channelings eight years later, I *did* begin writing a book in three months. He talked about many things that seemed so far away in time, but now we're indeed on that very precipice of great change that Michael first spoke of many years ago in our time, as if just a moment ago. He gave me a preview of what would occur eight years later, as if there were no barrier of time, because, in fact, there is no "time" in the Heavenly realms.

My communication with Michael began on the morning of November 15, 2001, in the beautiful area where I lived with my family in New Mexico. While driving in the car with my children, we saw an unforgettable sight. The clouds were very low to the ground, well below the top of the Sandia Mountains, and the sun radiated golden light in the form of a starburst shining directly on

2

these low-lying clouds. Because we lived in the foothills, as we drove, we were above many of these clouds, and the sight was so surreal, like nothing we'd ever seen before. My children both expressed the thought that "It looks like Heaven on earth," and I felt they interpreted the scene perfectly. As it turned out, that sight and that phrase perfectly described the subject matter of my future book, which I was about to embark on that very day.

On that day, for the first time, I channeled Archangel Michael. In hindsight, I realize now that this beginning of my relationship with him would culminate in the writing of this book and other future work, and all for one purpose: to take my place among many others to stand up and assist in the co-creation of "Heaven on earth." I know now that I contracted for this mission, to be a channel of Archangel Michael's messages. On that morning of first contact, following a meditation, I wrote the words: "I'm feeling very unmotivated, but struggling with that feeling. I choose for great things to happen that will propel me on my path, in my work." After writing these words, this is what followed:

First, I felt hugged. Then my face was being gently moved around, guided in different directions for several minutes. I could feel subtle energy where it was being touched. I believed it was Archangel Michael. I had asked for obvious signs from the "unseen," promising not to be scared, and I was not disappointed.

I then asked out loud, "Archangel Michael, are you there?" For several minutes, I felt extreme pressure around my eyes and on the outer tip of my left ear. Then came the following words, which were repeated slowly and firmly to assure me I was "hearing" him correctly:

Hello Mary. I come to you on this day to show you the Light. The Light you are so deserving of. Bask in this Light and take ownership of it. For it is yours. You are dearly loved. Yes, you have raised your vibration high enough to hear my messages. You have done this. Yes, your life is about to change. You will know a peace you have never known. Dwell in this place. Mary, you must listen even when the message seems crazy or ridiculous. I assure you I only speak what is true. I only speak of love. I only speak of the highest good! You've passed. You've passed this long and difficult test. You are so loved, Mary. It is highly appropriate that you dwell only in the place you call love. You shine there. You shine like a beacon of light.

Could this be true? Or was I making this up in my mind? I asked that question again and again. Michael's words did not come through as a voice, but rather I had a knowingness of his message, as if he were speaking to my mind and I heard it in that way.

The very next day, I called for him. Again, I felt the strong sensations in my eyes, primarily in the inside corners, as well as in my third eye. Then came a tingling in my upper lip and lower nose area. I also felt he was holding my hands. And he said:

You are in a place of love. When we talk, you are cooperating with the higher dimensions, having found a way to open the door to higher communications. Only you could open this door, and you have by giving your full intent. You have jumped the highest hurdle. And now, just relax and see what you created. You have been selected by the Order of Melchizedak to heed this calling. This is the very beginning of countless "conversations" we'll have together. You are justly honored for your work. You will fit into this new way of communication and it will become second nature to you. Do you feel me holding your hands? (yes.) I am right here with you and am always with you. I know you have many questions for me. I want to answer

4

all of them. And they will be answered in time. Be patient. Everything you need is yours. You are dearly loved, Mary.

On this day, while driving about thirty minutes away from home I saw the widest rainbow I've ever seen, and directly above my village. As I've come to learn, the skies do speak to us, and a rainbow or the shape of a cloud can often serve as a direct message. How do you know if it signifies a message for you or is just a pretty cloud or rainbow? Perhaps by considering what is going on in your life, or what you're thinking at the moment you see something telling from above. Sometimes, the message is revealing of the future. The same goes for what's occurring on the ground too. We'll get into that more later on.

When Michael mentioned the Order of Melchizedak, I didn't really understand exactly what he meant, but it somehow resonated deeply within me. As I learned at www.melchizedekusa.com, the Order of Melchizedak is described as being "composed of evolved beings who have dedicated themselves to the work of promoting spiritual growth wherever that is possible. It is the one true Spiritual Priesthood."

Michael went on to describe what our work would be about.

After three months of getting to know each other, your book writing days begin. You and I are bonded for life. These arrangements sound grandiose to you, don't they? But, oh, my angel, get used to this. Get used to happiness. Get used to having an angel by your side now and always and in every way! Are you surprised, dear one? You shouldn't be. This had been part of the plan for so long. Speak to me anytime. I am always here and will always answer you.

Are you still feeling alone? You won't feel so alone when you always feel me around. (I feel him moving my head around again.) *So do you like this arrangement? You ought to. You helped plan it. It was the most significant contract you ever made. You just asked me about books. Oh, yes, my dear, you are going to write plenty of books and, yes, it's all part of the contract. Through the information you impart, you will help usher in the new age of humanity. So celebrate this, for this is what you've waited for, for so long, Mary.*

No longer do I doubt having "signed" a contract for this work, prior to this incarnation. Allow me to backtrack to something that happened on October 2, 1994, something that catapulted me into a spiritual transformation in a single moment, and marked the true beginning of my conscious spiritual path in this life. In the weeks before, I was suffering from a deep depression to the point where I was on my knees begging God to help me, and help me He did. I began telepathically receiving profound messages and articulating words and thoughts that could not possibly be my own. I believed I was speaking with God.

Then on this particular day, I voiced the following words without thinking them; they just came out of my mouth: "Am I chosen?" A white light, what could be none other than Divine Light, came into my right eye. A sense of peace and love and inner knowing washed over me as all my senses tuned into this miraculous Light, through which I could barely see. I intuitively felt I was indeed chosen as one of the millions of messengers who are helping to awaken spirituality on earth (a role I would later learn is popularly referred to as a "Lightworker"). Needless to say, I came out of my depression immediately.

We each have the grandest support by our side, and we also have the ability to channel our angels and Archangels and even God, purely with intent and remaining open to the way the messages will come through. There is

6

nothing special about me. In fact, my ability to channel has not come easily. With the new energies, and as the veil between Heaven and earth thins, it will only become easier for us all.

Michael continued:

How many times have you held a baby in your arms and wondered what it is like to have that freedom of being? Well, that is just what you have. You are so free in every move you make. Bask in that freedom and let loose of the confines you put yourself in. It is highly appropriate behavior in the new energy. Do this with your thinking too. Hold freedom in your heart because then and only then can you fly. This isn't so easy for you to do because your natural habit is to put restraints on yourself. Let go of this, and you will know a new kind of joy. Remember this always.

No one can know us better than an angel, who knows our every thought, feeling, and experience. Michael was right about the restraints I put on myself. I was the only one holding myself back, and I needed this push to break through the mold I cast onto myself.

I know that many can relate to this, wanting to break free of the self-imposed restraints that hold us back. Once that impetus presents itself—whether a teacher, healer, inspirational message, meditation, encouraging friend, honest self-talk, or an Archangel comes along—and the light bulb goes on, there's no turning back and the world of possibilities is suddenly open to you. You get out of your own way and start living the life you were born to live. But there is no need to go it alone, as there is much help available to all of us.

As we step into our magnificence, we tap into who we really are. Once we follow our intended life's path, then our soul, our angels (with our request), and the Universe with its miraculous and constant flow of synchronicities, will step in to help light the way. We suddenly find ourselves with the right contacts, right opportunities, and everything falls into place. We need only trust and, thus, allow.

Let us say that on this day you favor a windy day. This may not be true, however, let us just say. And the wind comes along and destroys all that you worked on. Would you be upset at the wind? Let's take it a step further. Let's say you wished for the sun to shine instead. The sun comes and dries up all your fruit and vegetables. Are you upset at the sun? Now, in truth, you have asked God to come into your life and assume His will. Should you not expect some turbulence? All forces, forces of nature and the God force, are very powerful. You can't expect them not to wreck a little havoc in order to make change occur. Can you? That is what happened to you these last seven years. Havoc and turmoil resided alongside you. These were necessary for your growth. Can you deny this? Open your heart and accept this, embrace it in fact, for it was the only way for you to get to this place. And I know you're glad you did. Show the world how you can triumph over despair. And how you can feel God's comfort throughout the process.

This particular message delivered to me on a personal level years ago continues to speak to what is going on right now on a global level, during these most challenging times. As we are craving peace in our world, and, ultimately, the creation of our Heaven on earth, for that to manifest, many things have been knocked up, down, and sideways. In adversity—and this includes devastating war, our crumbling economy, neglect and poisoning of our environment, etc.—there is always opportunity. Greed, corruption, dishonesty, and oppression, are in a free fall. Havoc and turmoil are residing alongside us. Yet, we shall triumph over our present despair. We *will* create Heaven on earth. And we will feel God's comfort throughout the process.

Never in the history of mankind have humans been able to traverse through such remarkable feats. Never have humans been so ready to make change happen for the good of the Universe. It is rare to find such a dichotomy of intermingling souls working for and against the change. This was all to be expected. Everything is just as it is meant to be. When you look outside your window, you see destruction and unending chaos all over the world. What we see is a beautiful dichotomy of fixed beliefs and open hearts. The open hearts will win in the end. It is quite refreshing to know there are unseen forces at work here. You all need the help, but it cannot be done without you. How many times must we tell you all how much you are loved before you believe us?

"I believe you."

Be gentle with yourself for you have gone through so much. But now you can relax. Oh, Mary, you can honestly relax now. Just take a seat and enjoy the joyous ride. You will purposefully connect with your soul. Isn't that what you've wanted for so long, to be in constant connection with your soul? Well that's exactly what you'll be doing. You'll be with you. It will be a grand and glorious reunion.

This is increasingly happening right now, this experience of getting in closer touch with who I really am. As I review Michael's words of long ago, I feel the excitement and wonder of what it will be like when we all connect with our souls, when we all have this blessed reunion with our true selves. When we fully connect with our souls, and find the illusions melting away, we'll have peace on earth—and, thus, Heaven on earth.

Soon after I began my spiritual journey about sixteen years ago, I began to hear a sound in my head, and I still

9

hear this sound every day of my life. Michael refers to the meaning of this sound, and how he uses it to communicate with me.

The spiritual sound you have heard for the past seven years is another means by which I communicate. You ask if that sound has been me these past seven years. Specifically, it is like a cord that connects you to us and is your gateway to the higher dimensions, not just me. So I can use the sound to penetrate your consciousness ever since you gave your intent. I speak to you through an interdimensional level of communication that your higher self can understand. The higher self then communicates with you on a conscious level to incorporate my teachings.

Michael then went on to address my insecurities regarding my channeling abilities:

When the time is right, I will increase the speed of which I communicate to you. You want that to happen now, but that is not possible. It will take some time to get to that level. You see, it's like throwing you into some marathon without all the practice and building up you need in order to perform. It will happen soon enough. Enjoy the way it is right now. Try to imagine yourself having the clear communication you so desire.

Yes, to answer you, in time you will be able to "see" me as well as other interdimensional beings. Again, you can imagine this, as well, while being happy with your present situation.

A few days later he spoke more of interdimensional sight:

Did you know that you will all see Heaven? With your new eyes, you will see interdimensionally. This will scare some, bring hope to others, and create a new template of the new possibilities any being can behold. You won't be scared; rather you will be delighted and intrigued.

10

The news kept getting better and better.

There is magic between us now.

After typing the previous words with my eyes shut (since I usually shut my eyes while typing channeled messages), I opened my eyes and these words were gone! They were no longer on the computer screen, so I retyped them.

You are a firm believer in the miracles of life, and you are now going to partake more and more in them. They will manifest themselves in so many different situations in your life. This is part of the new energy, so awaken to this fact. Yes, you and I working together is miraculous in itself. It is crucial that you just allow all the magic and miracles to happen between us. Don't resist anything as all is in order. We have taken just the first steps together in our long journey together. Release all concerns and prepare for a new and miraculous life.

I then told Michael that, "As much as I want to accept this, I admit I wish for clearer messages to prove to myself this is you."

Then put the computer down and I will show you this is me.

I put the computer down and, immediately, I could feel Archangel Michael, not "around me," but more like he was now sharing my body. I felt this especially regarding my face, and most acutely with regard to my facial expressions. It's hard to find exactly the right words to describe an experience like this, so let me simply say that the feeling was quite intense and I knew that the expressions on my face were Michael's, and not my own.

Our spirits are intertwined; I'm joined with you in your physical vessel. Can you tell me you don't feel different? We will continue the channel being this close and you will hear me much clearer. This is our future. This is how we will speak. Although I won't take over your conscious self and speak through you, rather I will join you and you will remain fully conscious and transcribe my message. Isn't this clearer for you? Are you delighted? Feel this, feel what is happening right now and make a firm intent if you wish for this to continue in this way. I told you we'd be bonded for life. Did you think we'd be this close?

The facial sensations were especially strong, although I felt sensations reaching all the way down to my toes.

You are making great headway today. Do you feel the extra energy? Do you feel the feelings of oneness with me? We are one. Allow your energies to mesh with mine. It is such a pleasant time to be with you like this. As you head into the fifth dimension, you will feel this connected all the time. This is your journey, your ticket to the fifth dimension. I will guide you there, my angel. There you will reside in peace, tranquility, and an ecstasy you've never known. You feel consumed with thoughts about third dimensional things, lately. The time you spend with me is your break from it; a much needed break. We can be at this place together whenever you request, for it will be so. Do you see the difference? Do you feel the difference? I think so. Is it like you've just re-birthed yourself into an angel?

Like many others, I was dealing with various physical discomforts that come with vibrational shifts, as physical discomfort is a common side effect of these ongoing shifts. I say ongoing because we are making small shifts or improvements all the time, as we continue to raise our vibrations. Michael, aware of what I've been personally dealing with, brought the subject up on what was a particularly difficult day for me:

Just allow for these minor discomforts to occur. They seem strong, but they aren't causing you harm. They are necessary for your evolution, Mary. There is much to be

12

celebrated here. Can you imagine experiencing this without understanding what is behind it? Many souls are experiencing this at this time and will in the future. That is one way how you will help them by expressing your personal experience with the discomforts, the aches and pains, the low energy, and so on.

I felt better knowing that there was a good reason for my aches and pains. At this point, it wasn't even three weeks since I began channeling Michael before he gave me a taste of what the messages in this book would be like:

Isn't it time to try out your new wings, author? Let us write our first message for the masses.

Dear readers: Make way for a new life unlike that you've ever lived in your many lives, your endless incarnations. This one is so special and unique for it is the first time you have full realization of who you really are while existing in a physical vessel. This just so happens to be a product of countless of beings, on both sides of the veil, working to provide enlightenment for the greater whole. Can you deny that this is occurring? Can you deny that you yourself are changing? Sound the Clarion Call and mark this moment in time as the moment you claim your Divinity. Then show your Light for all to see, so they too may access the Light. In this new world, you will help one another. You might say your priorities will change. You will no longer accept greed or hate to motivate, for these behaviors and emotions won't work anymore. Rather, love will be the domineering force in your lives. Your success stories will come from those of you who practice love of self, love of others, love of the earth, and the love of God. When you participate in these acts of love, you find your Divine self.

What perfect words and what a perfect time in history to hear them. Many of us have grown tired and weary

13

from all the difficulties and challenges we have continually faced. That is why having a support system is so important, to work with others to help us through the shifts. When we step into our purpose, the Universe responds by bringing not only the ideal situations, opportunities, and people to help us succeed in our missions, but also those who can provide us with loving, emotional support. Michael explained eight years ago what is happening now in my own life as I begin to write this book.

So, Mary Soliel, how is it that you are going to provide the material for this book? By channeling messages from me and incorporating your own life experiences throughout. This will prove to be a very effective tool for many humans who are approaching their path to their Divinity.

You are on the brink of finding out just who will support you, just who will be the human element responsible for providing you with the emotional and psychological support you need to succeed in this endeavor.

Michael was so right. I continually meet people who provide me with emotional and psychological support, and I find myself providing others with the same. By supporting each other, we're all achieving our goals and are consciously making efforts to help each other succeed. There are many Lightworkers involved in this work, all charged with different aspects of the mission. And many, like myself, are charged with channeling information and getting it out there in book form. Why have so many channelers/authors? Because as each of us brings forward the information—often similar in meaning, but in our own unique way and style—readers find a channel they each resonate with, and the messages, thus, reach more people.

The more I focus on all that is good, such as the beautiful support I receive from fellow Lightworkers as I continue my work, the better off I am. I'm still being tested with negative energies from people who are aligned differently from me. Michael gave me some wise advice on this subject:

Prepare yourself for that which doesn't mesh with your new consciousness. By that I mean, don't allow negative energies to inflict wounds on you any longer. Accept the Light and move past your third dimensional existence. You are like a new flower that has shown itself amidst the old. Take refuge in your own garden and don't allow the old to change your beauty or uniqueness. Collect the rays of sunlight to make you grow brighter and stronger. You are a beautiful flower, Mary Soliel.

It is of vital importance now that you take special care and attention to what you feed yourself, meaning your thoughts, feelings, actions, and words, as well as food. Think light, think bright, and make decisions and affirmations that will resonate to your constantly growing higher vibrations. Before you ingest food, put your hand over it and bless it. I will be blessing it simultaneously. It will symbolize the sacred act of purposeful eating. Eat only that which you need to sustain you. I will help. You can call on me for all your decision-making. I will help you dissolve the unnecessary weight you carry. You no longer need to search for love through food. You will learn to access your love from God and no longer turn to food for the illusion of comfort it provides. You will taste of God's love, which is sweeter than any dessert, heartier than any meal, and is always plentiful and bountiful. This is the new Mary, the incarnation of Mary Soliel. This is my pledge and promise that if you follow my lead, my direction, you will be the physical expression of who you really are!

Having been overweight much of life, rarely have I felt

that I look like who I really am. My weight issues stem from so many sources and reasons; for instance, from past lives when I starved to death and my subconscious memories made sure I was never to starve again. Add to that my childhood relationships that ripped away at my self-esteem. But it is clear to me now that the greatest reason, which Michael describes, is to fill a void that nothing on this third dimensional existence can fill—an intense loneliness that only God can fill.

Childhood is such a difficult time for so many of us, and experiences from our childhood do affect us in ways we often don't fully realize. While growing up, I experienced incredible parental and sibling love in my family life. As is most critical to the well-being of any child, my parents were a constant source of unconditional love, but there were also difficulties I endured from others throughout my childhood that knocked down my self-esteem again and again. Michael refers to this in order to help others heal from wounds inflicted in the past:

Take heart, for that which caused you great distress now proves meaningful. Do you know what I'm talking about? I'm speaking of your childhood. The difficulties you endured are a testament to your strength and character. You allowed the contract to be fulfilled and now you reap the benefits. Do you realize this? Are you aware that what is happening now is a direct result of what happened then? The hardship was necessary and brought you to this place. Your self-esteem was destroyed so you can now claim it, and claim it in a big way. This is rainbow time, so to speak. The storm of your life, which began with those childhood hardships, has now come to a close and the rainbow is setting over you.

You can assist others in getting to their rainbow time. It is vital for them to face their past, as it is a vital and ne-

cessary part of human evolution. It will challenge many to break free of their childhoods, their past. It will offer hope for those who lost hope. It will convey the need for conscious living and will restore broken ties with the Creator.

Somewhere in your brain is a flame that is growing thicker and brighter. It is the Light in you that can transform and transmute that which no longer serves you in your grand existence. Honor this most sacred part of you. Imagine it growing and filling your whole body and outside your body. Embrace its beauty.

As I come into your space, Mary, I see that a darkness has left you. In that void is none other than Light. You have successfully transmuted the dark into Light. In these final days of your cleansing, you will see a surge in opportunities to create much more Light. Take heed of them and continue to access the Light from the higher dimensions. You are immersed in your progress even if you don't think so. The continuing weight gain, the frustrations, and the concerns are all necessary. Do you see the Light at the end of the tunnel now? It is there, just one more phase to trudge through. Has it occurred to you that you are in the company of many on my side? You are being watched and cheered on. You give us hope that others will follow in your footsteps. When it's very quiet, ask for those who are with you to make themselves known. They are waiting for this opportunity to communicate with you. You can hear their words of encouragement and praise, as well. Allow yourself to hear these messages—messages you are so deserving of. You are loved beyond measure.

It did not take long to see who else wanted to communicate with me. When Michael finished speaking the message above, I immediately said, "I give my full intent for any high being to communicate with me at this time." And here's who answered my call:

17

I Am Metatron, and I come to you in love and peace. I have watched you without your being aware. I am fully cooperating with Archangel Michael to help bring you to a state of ascension. You have come far. Do not dwell in anything negative at this time. Your purity is shining forth and beaming currents of love and Light. You are embarking on the path of a rainbow. You will soon be filled with joys you never thought possible. Love yourself for the great being you are. Hold yourself in the highest esteem and praise yourself for the path you've traveled. I, Metatron, am with you always.

Dear violet being, I Am Chamuel, your master teacher of love and compassion. Whenever you have thought it possible that love can prevail in all situations, I have encouraged you on. Love can surpass all, and that has been my main message. You have endured much heartbreak in your life, all while desiring to give much love, ever since you were a young girl. Your rewards will be great for all the love and compassion you've instilled in others. This is the promise of the Universe. You will be clearly blessed. Peace be with you.

While I had no expectations of who was going to communicate with me, I was thrilled when Metatron and Chamuel introduced themselves. And I must say, I was not prepared for who came through next:

I stand in one corner of the Universe in full view of the Light you have anchored in the earth. This is your Higher Self, Mary Soliel. Yes, I Am you, and I foresaw and have seen the grand shift you're making toward the higher dimensions. I speak to you all the time. I am guiding you and helping you on your very significant path. I Am the filter through which Archangel Michael speaks to you. There are no limits to where you can take your abilities now. Open your heart to the possibilities. You can com-

18

municate with me like this whenever you wish. Can you foresee that our relationship will grow closer? I am your link to the higher realms, Mary Soliel. Through me, you have access to paradise. Stay the course and miracles will abound.

Your body is tired now, but it won't stay that way. You will one day have the energy of a very young woman. You will need this for your work. It would be practical for you to visualize and imagine your future so that you can help bring it into reality. Things will move quickly for you. Remember, soon your difficulties will be over and you will sit in amazement.

And then, Michael was back, and his next message made my heart beat fast:

Take heed of this very important message, dear one. You are standing right in front of a new door. When you open it, you will find yourself in a new dimension. Yes, the fifth dimension. The time has come for you to show your Divinity to yourself and to the world. You will break into a new portal and be surrounded with golden opportunities. This isn't fluff or make believe words. This is real and it is I, Archangel Michael, speaking them to you. Life will begin anew and you will adopt a myriad of new skills and passions. Of course, our work together will be most significant, but there will be changes that will surprise and delight you in your life.

Let me elaborate a bit. The time has come where you will no longer question anything you do. You will know what is necessary at all times, and you won't second-guess. When the time is right, new people will come into your life, and you will enjoy many different relationships. You will have unlimited access to my realm. You will get guidance and support at any time you wish. You will be constantly infused with the Light and will no longer have such physical difficulty accepting it. Life, in general, will get much more interesting!

Dear Mary Soliel, the Light in you is shining forth, and you're starting to get a glimpse of the realm of possibilities before you. Your true devotion to God is shining forth. There is a stream of information going through you, information you are unaware of on a conscious level, but which will eventually show itself. This information is getting your mind-set ready for your evolution, for your first steps into the new dimension, the fifth dimension. You have an intuitive sense that this is going on. Meditate on your crown chakra, and see the information coming through. See it as light packets of information being welcomed into your being. Shelf all that is no longer a necessary part of your being and allow the new information to guide you higher and higher. Oh, Mary Soliel, you are honored so. If you could only see who is in my company now as I speak to you. The waiting is almost over. You soon shall see.

You amaze me by your utter willingness to adopt a new "position" as a channel for me. You are by no means scared of what our work together will bring, and you must realize how unusual this is for a human. You are right to not be scared; nevertheless, you are praised for your bravery. You see, my dear angel, you are under my supreme protection; and although you will meet many challenges, you will be strongly protected, guided, and loved. You cannot even fathom what is being done for you from my side. Hold onto this truth with all your spirit. Imagine my hand always there to hold, giving you support and strength. It is always there.

Nothing is more comforting to me than knowing my angels are with me, feeling their presence, and even their touch. The recognition and feeling of our angels' presence is a gift available to us all, and this topic will be elaborated on later in this book.

Mary Soliel, you have come so far. You are now this beacon of Light who has traversed the greatest and most challenging path of her many lifetimes and has surpassed expectations. Yes, dear angel in hiding all these years, you have leaped through layers and layers of adversity, pain, isolation, et cetera, and are nearing the finishing line. Beyond that line are all your finest dreams. Don't turn back now, just keep going and before you know it, you will reach the end for a new beginning. The fifth dimension is what I'm talking about, dear one, and the new colors are going to look quite good on you.

The number 22 has had much meaning and significance for you, especially these last couple of years. You know that 22 is a master number. You indeed are turning into a master, a master on earth. Do you have any idea what this means, bright angel? It is your greatest achievement. It is the culmination of ages of planning and the time is here. Behold, you are getting ready to assume your new role within the Christ-consciousness. Nothing will ever be the same and you will bless this truth. Start noticing the colors.

You are walking taller now, as you should. Do you feel different? (yes, I do.) You're starting to feel more comfortable "wearing" more Light. This is a quick and final phase. Stay on course and you will reap numerous rewards. You are young and you have years of service to this world. By holding firm to your mission, you will move many mountains. I'll be with you every step of the way.

Again, we meet at a glorious time, a time of harvesting. You, Mary Soliel, are reaping the rewards of your spiritual achievement. Yes, Mary, this is the time of your life. Grasp this truth and hold on for a life beyond your imaginings.

*God is pleased, so very pleased with you. He wants to make
an example of you for many of His other children. His love
for you is filling up every empty space within you, especially in your heart. Cover yourself with the warmth of God,
for He has created in you a new existence. It is filled with
love and more love. In it, you will exceed your greatest
expectations of yourself. You will harness the God-given
energy you've sought for so many lifetimes. Bring it in,
Mary, bring it in. That's right. Let it transform your whole
body; each cell, each organ, each drop of life-giving blood.
See the Light pulsating throughout and transmuting any
darkness left. There are others who want to speak to you at
this time.*

I was deeply honored and humbled by the presence of
the who came through next:

*Dear Mary Soliel, I Am Mother Mary, and I've heard
your cries for love. Allow me to take your sadness away
and replace it with the love of Christ, my Son. Heaven is
showering over you now. You have an ocean of love to fill
your beautiful being. Take it and soar with it to new
places, new journeys, and new beginnings. Heaven is
watching. Heaven is waiting for you to drink of the Light
to overflowing. And when you do so, you will bring others
to the same well. This is the beginning of the greatest
journey of your lives. Find your treasure, share your treasure, and your dream will become reality.*

Before I had a chance to digest the words from Mother
Mary, Archangel Gabriel made himself known with the
following message:

*This is Archangel Gabriel, the master angel of mercy
and compassion, and I applaud you Mary Soliel. You have
stepped onto new ground, new territory, and your life will
never be the same. There are many here on my side anxious
to speak to you, but only a few will be allowed. Accept the*

reality and the beauty of all that is happening. You must hold onto your truth, just as you always have, because there will always be ripples with change; and you are changing very quickly, blessed angel on earth. We're all watching you anxiously and stand waiting to greet you when you get to the point that we can meet. That is just footsteps away. Can you feel it, Angel? Start imagining what this will be like. This is the way it was once and soon will be. Your life is so much more significant than you realize and you will soon see what I mean. We applaud the great strides you've made and honor you greatly. I am watching you too; just look for the signs to show you. You can't imagine how far from alone you really are. Go in peace and remember what I've told you.

As soon as Gabriel finished his message, another entity came through and he felt familiar:

Hello dear angel, I was your teacher at one point in your present life. Not too long ago, in fact. I am simply known as John. You're feeling emotion well up in you because you know I was once your guide. I had to leave you and now you're feeling this reunion on a deep level. You have come far, Mary, and your future is bright. You gift others by being in service, and all is going perfectly according to plan. Embrace all that you are and how far you have come. I am watching you.

As mentioned, anyone who channels will receive extraordinary information about whom they really are. No one is better than another, and I strongly encourage you, if you haven't already, to channel your own messages. There are many resources that teach how to channel (please refer to my channeling video on the "MarySoliel" channel on youtube.com). It is a simple process that begins with intent and awareness. We all channel, but when you are conscious of it, this is where the beauty begins.

CHAPTER 2

My Connection to Michael Grows

I n my first book, *I Can See Clearly Now: How Synchronicity Illuminates Our Lives,*[1] I shared the awe-inspiring synchronicities that revealed my connection to Archangel Michael. I repeat some of these stories in this chapter in order to explain how the magical beginnings of this relationship mirrored to me that I had truly contracted to work with Michael. As previously published:

[1] Soliel, Mary. *I Can See Clearly Now: How Synchronicity Illuminates Our Lives.* Lincoln: iUniverse, 2008.

My greatest spiritual blessing is my conscious relationship with a particular Archangel. In July of 2001, I became aware that an angel was communicating with me. His name was Thomas, and I channeled that he was preparing me for communication with Archangel Michael. Surely this was in my imagination, a statement I made in my mind countless times in the succeeding months. However, in November of that year, I began to receive information from Archangel Michael. I channeled many messages over the next several weeks through a psychic, telepathic hearing, in my case. It's as if you're hearing words, but it is through a knowingness and without sounds.

Therefore, please note that where I write things such as "I hear Michael say" or "Michael told me," I refer not to a sound, but to a knowingness—a type of telepathic hearing that does not involve my ears. I'm not normally the type of clairaudient who hears actual sounds with my physical ears. In the beginning, I questioned and doubted much of the information I was receiving.

One evening, while taking a long drive from Las Cruces to Albuquerque in late December, I channeled Michael the whole way home. At one point, he said he had a name for me. In my mind, I "saw" the letters S-O-L-I-E-L. I asked out loud, "So-leel?" "No," I heard him say, and then I knew that it was phonetically pronounced "Sol-ee-ehl." Was this really happening? I thought it was my mind playing tricks on me.

Michael told me to find the numerology of both his and my name on the numerology chart when I returned home, which I did. I found that Archangel

Michael's name was a 12. To my surprise and delight, Mary Soliel was also a 12. That was the beginning of 12:12 synchronicities to occur in connection with Michael. By the way, I'm writing this chapter on 12/12/06, in his honor, but that isn't a surprise, is it?

In the Spring of 2002, my kids and I visited a park near Las Cruces for an overnight stay so we could do some serious rock hounding, an ideal family outing for us nature lovers. As I'm writing this, I recognize the commonality that I've been to the Las Cruces area only twice, and both times were very relevant in affirming my connection to Michael. The day before we had left on the trip, Michael asked me to be aware of a sign from him among the rocks. When we were a couple of hours into our treasure searches, I was frustrated that I couldn't find the sign. I was on a constant lookout for it, yet nothing appeared meaningful. However, the sign would actually find me, as it turned out, and through none other than my children.

My son found a rock and excitedly said, "Mom! Look at this!" Scott placed into my hand a unique and beautiful piece of volcanic rock. I was speechless when I immediately realized it looked just like a flower; each of the five petals and the center were bubbled. Michael said in several channels that I'm "a flower about to bloom."

Just a couple of seconds after Scott handed the rock to me, Karen, who was rarely curious about the time, especially when engrossed in an activity such as this, asked, "What time is it, Mom?" I looked at my watch. "It's 12:12!" I exclaimed with pure joy. Leave it to my beautiful kids to present my sign so perfectly; there was no need for me to frantically search for a sign that would actually find me at the most perfect moment in time. I then realized that I needed to trust in my ability to channel, but the truth is that I continued to question things I heard for several more months.

Until writing this book, I have shared my connection to Michael with very few. One of them was my friend, Kat, who was very familiar and comfortable with the idea of channeling. When I told her that Michael calls me "Soliel," she asked if I realized that sol means "sun" in Spanish. I knew that but for some reason I never really put it together. (I later learned that *sol* means "sun" in several other languages as well.)

He is calling me "angel of the sun" then, I said, because *iel* is the ending of many angels' names (such as Ariel, Gabriel, and Uriel). Why it took more than six months to come to that realization I don't know, but I think it was because it sounded so grandiose, and I don't feel any more special than the next person. But the fact is, we are *all* grandiose! We all are beautiful spiritual beings, so powerful beyond measure. Most of us are unaware of our magnificence and the fact that we each have access to our higher selves, our angels and Archangels, and the Heavenly realms. And every one of us has the ability to channel, as well, if we so desire.

One week after I accepted this new understanding of my name, my family left for a trip to Maui, in the summer of 2002. Just before we left, Michael told me that I would see a ring in Hawaii that I must have and wear, as a symbol of our bond.

Just as with the rock, I was looking too hard for the ring. I spent hours going into nearly every jewelry shop in Lahaina, with no luck. I just wanted a simple silver band with a simple symbol of a sun but couldn't find anything I liked or that was my style. When was I going to learn? I finally realized I needed to patiently allow Michael to "present" it to me in his own way, even though I was so excited to find the symbol. As it turned out, my connection to Michael was even more significant than I had allowed myself to believe.

About halfway through the trip, I felt a strange urge to go down to the hotel gift shop during a lazy afternoon. I dislike touristy items and am not a shopper by any means unless I'm shopping for books, but I followed the feeling and told my family I was going to take a quick look there. My life would never be the same after that visit. What would occur was the most profound synchronicity I have ever experienced—beyond my wildest imagination.

I walked around the store, clueless as to why I was there. The store did not sell any rings, so it wasn't for that reason. I later realized that I channeled my need to be there, that Michael had surely whispered it to me. I eventually walked over to the handful of books on display, a collection of only seven different publications.

One immediately caught my eye. It was about the prophet Nostradamus, called *Prophecies for America*[2], but it was a new interpretation of his predictions, so it grabbed my attention. I thought it was incredibly strange that there would be a book about

---

[2] Ovason, David. *Prophecies for America*. New York: Avon, 2001.

29

Nostradamus, one of just a handful of books being sold in a luxury hotel in Maui. I wondered how many people would actually desire reading about catastrophic prophecies while sunbathing in paradise. And how many hotels in the whole world were displaying it? Just one? But the Universe made sure I saw this book while visiting the "Island of the Sun."

Holding the book in my hands, I opened it to a certain page. My eyes went directly to a paragraph that referred to the Archangels who were said to rule specific periods of time in history. It said, "We are living under the rulership of Michael, the angel of the Sun." *Michael! The angel of the Sun!*

I closed the book and went wide-eyed, feeling as if I'd gone out of my body. How could this be happening to me, a little speck of a being on this planet? Then I heard Michael tell me to move a few feet over. It was a knowingness to just move where he wanted me to be, and so I did. He then wanted me to open the book again, to that very page. I found it immediately, and a drop of water fell right onto that paragraph, covering those very words.

Above me, I saw some condensation at the edge of a ceiling air vent; I had been moved so that I'd be standing at the right spot and the drop would fall on the right place, reinforcing the message in case I somehow tried to explain it away. The fact is, I could never question my connection to Michael again. I could never question the connections we all have to angels and Archangels. The veil between Heaven and earth thinned to nearly nothing during this most astounding moment of my life.

As if that weren't enough, when I went to

purchase the book, the clerk who sold it to me had the name "MaryChris" displayed on her name badge. To me, this symbolized my recognizing the Divine ("Christ") part of me. From the time Michael gave me my new name, he was mirroring Divine connection in miraculous ways. It was then and there that I needed to release the illusion of my separateness from the Divine—the same illusion that needs to be released from *all* of us.

Synchronicity is what is perfect in this world. How impeccable was it that Kat, just a week before this miracle, helped me see past my insecurities so I could embrace the true meaning of my name? Then this meaning was perfectly validated by a miraculous chain of events that resulted in my ultimate transformation.

In my dozens of trips to many different bookstores over the years since this book about Nostradamus was published in October, 2001, I never saw that book, before or since that day in the hotel gift shop, except in its now prominent place in my personal library. But there it was at the perfect time and the perfect place, amazingly situated among a tiny display of just six other books.

The evening before we left Maui, my family and I went to a mall to pick up dinner at a food court. I kept feeling drawn to it when driving by, even though I'm not at all a fan of shopping malls. As we entered the building, we walked right next to a jewelry stand. There it was. The ring was just what I'd envisioned, a simple sterling silver band with a simple figure of the sun—perfect. The ring found me! In what seemed to take about two minutes, I spotted, tried on, and bought the ring, just like that. No wonder I'd felt so driven to visit that mall (thank you for the whispers, dear Michael). I have been wearing my ring from Michael every day since, with thoughts of our connection every time I put it on.

Two years after this life-altering trip to Maui, I divorced my husband. In the few months preceding it, I considered legally changing my name to "Mary Soliel" but with much anguish. My intense fear of what others would think of me if I changed my last name to something totally unexpected was clouding my objectivity. I chose to confide in my healer about my connection with Michael and the related synchronicities. I had already made an appointment to see her, and I would ask her to help me see clearly regarding this issue.

Prior to my appointment on a typically sunny day in New Mexico, I was driving my kids to school. Just the night before, I'd told my son about my relationship with Archangel Michael for the first time. If I was going to change my name, I needed to first share my connection to Michael with my kids, so I first told Scott.

As I had thoughts and concerns in my mind about changing my name, I turned the corner, looked up into the sky, and gasped out loud at what I saw. My daughter, who knew nothing about the "angel of the sun" synchronicities yet, said, "Look at the sun, Mom! There are angel wings around it!" I looked at my son, and he was as wide-eyed as I was, having just learned of my relationship with Michael the night before. There were two clouds in the form of perfect angel wings on each side of the sun, and I had my question answered. I didn't need to go outside of myself and search for an answer. *Gulp.* The worries about what my parents, friends, or acquaintances would think about my new name paled in comparison to my newly found courage and realization that I was destined and guided to carry this name.

Chapter 3

An Introduction to the Unknown Light

On November 21, 2001, Archangel Michael woke me to talk about something so special, and it was a preview of our future. He spoke the words, "Liquid Light." Even though I'm just beginning to write this book eight years later, I know that part of it will be about this new gift that will eventually be recognized as our greatest reward as we enter the Golden Age. I asked Michael to explain exactly what it is:

Oh, my angel, Liquid Light is quite possibly the most extraordinary thing that you can imagine. It is the purest concentration of energy in the form of Light. It comes from

God and is available to all that is. That doesn't mean everyone can access it right now. It can be accessed by those of high enough vibration who can handle the effects of its powerful force. It allows beholders to think, feel, and express Light and only the Light. It is appropriate to offer it back to God for it is fluid and will always return to you. There is no reason to fear it even though it will at first seem foreign to you. You will adjust and come to treasure it more than anything you've ever beheld.

It will create sensations and feelings beyond description. You will never be without it, to answer your question. It will replace many of your physical needs. You could one day, how shall I say, purely live off of it. It is like a tonic with miraculous qualities, filling every part of your body and every cell. From the outside you may seem the same, but, oh, from the inside you will feel a peace, joy, and an ecstasy you've never known. Imagine, it will be there for you one hundred percent of the time. I say this is true. Oh, yes, it will change your life.

"Will it improve my communication with you, so that I may 'hear' you better?"

Yes, dear heart. You will hear me better, but that's just the beginning. This is the single most significant step toward becoming a new human that you will make. It is the tonic that will have a grand and immediate impact on your evolution toward becoming a fifth dimensional human being.

"Will the books that we'll write together discuss this property?"

You are right on target. See how psychic you are? You don't realize. Try and grasp this reality. You are going to bring in new and startling information to help mankind adjust to the new era you're fast approaching.

"I don't mean to sound vain, but will Liquid Light melt

this extra weight I'm carrying?"

Of course it will, Mary. On some level you've known this. Don't worry about sounding vain; we understand your concerns. You have every right to want to feel who you are again. This weight has weighed so heavily on you. It absolutely was necessary to fulfill this present part of your mission. Take heed; you will feel good again in every way imaginable.

"Will one need to continually ask for the Liquid Light, or will it just automatically and continuously flow through us?"

The Light energy will be tapped on a continual basis without your realizing it.

During a separate channeling session, which just happened to be on a particularly difficult day for me, he said:

There will come a time when the old you is merely a memory and you will honor your past self. I know you're feeling out of sorts today. That is because you are making this grand shift and your body knows it. Every cell in your body knows it, and it is normal and expected that the body would resist change. Let us together affirm, "I fully accept the new energy of Light that will infiltrate my being. It is a gift from God."

Needless to say, I was so glad that Michael addressed this issue, because while some of us are very aware of what is commonly referred to as "Ascension Symptoms," others who are experiencing them may not understand what's happening to them. Some common symptoms are that we are often tired, achy, and sometimes don't even want to get out of bed. Some of us feel out of sync with our very selves, perhaps even feeling depressed at times. The passage above can help us look at how we perceive these difficulties with new eyes.

These symptoms confirm the changes we're experiencing on a cellular level. So I suggest using the affirmation above, really feeling the words when speaking them, to help make this shift as easy as possible for both our bodies as well as our emotional states of being. (You can search "Ascension Symptoms" on Google to learn more. Always see a doctor if you have medical concerns.)

There is no way to know right now at this moment just how much your life will change literally overnight. But trust me and don't be afraid, you will be well pleased.

As we raise our vibrations, we continue the repetitive process of making shifts of change again and again. I know that something has shifted within me many times over recent years as I have raised my own vibration, but most especially right now. This is no race, and how and when we feel each shift is no competition, nor is it a reflection of one person being better than the other. There are so many dynamics involved, and the timing is in perfect order for each individual.

When Michael began sharing these descriptions of Liquid Light back in 2001, he asked me to "try not to talk of this to others for they will not understand." I kept my word until now, because now is the right time.

Soon after I first reunited with my precious binder filled with those beginning messages from Michael, I felt compelled to write a short article about them, and did so in November of 2009. It took a lot of courage for me to do this. What would people think of this Liquid Light? What would people think of me for writing about it? I trusted that I needed to go out on a limb, and, in fact, I needed to get used to doing just that. I even sent an email out to friends and colleagues suggesting that if there was one article I wish they'd read of mine, it was this one.

What happened after I sent that email greatly surprised me. I received several responses, all from people resonating one way or another with Liquid Light! They either had just heard about it, were already interested in it, or were channeling it themselves. One new friend said he had heard of "Liquid Light" at a gathering once back in 1983, and hadn't heard of it again until this very article!

I shared these messages with a close friend by phone one night, and she responded that the term, "Liquid Light," was new to her. However, the very next day, I received a text message from her explaining that she just started reading a mystery novel and it mentioned "liquid light"! She knows, as I do, that there are no coincidences. She was receiving validation that this was real. I myself had only once seen Liquid Light referred to in an esoteric book I read, back in the mid-90s. Needless to say, I was astounded and overjoyed by the response.

Chapter 4

The New Messages from Michael

T he messages in this chapter were received beginning
on February 1, 2010. Six weeks earlier, my family
and I had moved into a new house, which gave me just
enough time to make a home and prepare to begin the
most important work of my life thus far—receiving messages from Archangel Michael for this very book. Most of
his messages were received in the wee hours when I was
most receptive and clear, and it was easier to keep my
conscious mind from getting in the way. Michael would
usually wake me by 4:30 every morning, although sometimes as early as 2:00 a.m. While fast asleep, I'd hear a

doorbell ring. The first couple of times this occurred, I would get up and see who was at the door at such a ridiculous hour. Of course, there was no one. It was Michael's way of waking me, inside my mind. I have to say it made me really chuckle except for those mornings I just wanted to sleep at least a little bit longer; even though I knew I'd usually be able to go back to sleep, after I finished my writing. Yes, angels can and do communicate with us through sound. They can make doorbells and telephones ring, in our minds or out loud, and they can get our attention in a variety of ways. What a funny way to wake up.

And so the new messages begin...

Dear Mary Soliel, angel of the sun. How can I tell you how much you are loved, how much everyone on your precious earth is loved? You would not believe how many of us are here in the Heavens supporting all of you, loving you, and helping you through these very difficult times. You are not alone. You are not without everything you need to endure the coming changes until one day you will find yourself in a new territory, a new energy, and a new everything. When that day comes, because there will one day be an immediate shift that will take you to new heights of living as a human being, you will be comprised of so much more Light than you are now. Does that scare you readers? Let it not be so! The best of your life, all your earthly lives, is yet to come. Only you can choose to dwell here. Only you can choose to adjust and reap the benefits of opening up your heart to a new way of being on this planet. You will be amazed by the beauty and love and opportunities that will abound. You will be surprised by the miracles that will occur on a daily basis! Little by little, you will get glimpses of what this will be like through this very book, but even this book can't tell the whole story, because it is so grand beyond human imagination. Listen to your heart and feel the truth of my words. You are all angels on earth. Your wings are growing. The time is now to delve deep into the understanding of who you really are. To know your soul and to make right with all that has happened in the past. Make peace with your former pain and hardships. Clear away the old and begin to accept that a new life for all is before you. Love each other throughout this process and live from your heart. See the beauty in all people, all of nature, all the ongoings that brought you to this point of transformation. Be in love with life, and, in your imagination, wrap your arms around this loving earth and give it a hug sending love from your heart right to its very core. I am Archangel Michael, your friend and protector.

There is so much we do not know as human beings. We don't have the capability to fully understand life as it is, let alone life as it will be in the very near future. This is why I've always been drawn to channeling ever since I began my spiritual path. Science isn't going to give us all the answers. But our angels can give us a much greater understanding.

We are spiritual pioneers together embarking on the unknown; scary to some, beyond exciting to others. In order to be successful pioneers, we need to embrace change, or at least learn to accept it. I've always felt that the only constant is change, but that couldn't be more true as it is for us now. And that philosophy is apropos both for today, and what we will greet with the new sun tomorrow.

The time is now to gather what no longer resonates to your changing vibrations and just release it. Most people don't like change, but change is what is happening and fast. Listen to your heart, and when you feel upset or discord with something, ask if it needs to be released. What behaviors do you want to release? What addictions do you want to let go of? Your angels can help you release your addictions, so ask them! What actions that used to be a part of your normal routine no longer feel right anymore? Is it time to set aside those ones that rob you of your energy or no longer seem useful, but have just become mere habits? Take a look at your life and consider those things that beg to be released: friends that no longer resonate with you, work that gives you no joy, foods that don't nurture you and actually harm you, entertainment that brings you a notch down your ladder of vibrational standing. The beauty of releasing things now is that it comes so much easier. When you make the decision to let go, you get the support of the Universe, and because you are at higher vibrations, your grip on attachments is lessening. I'm not suggesting you go give all your possessions away or go move to another country so you are completely starting anew. It is small, simple changes, one by one, which will grow into an overall change in you that supports the new energy. Don't bother thinking about it too much as it will just happen naturally once you set your intention. You will assume a broader understanding of who you are and who you are becoming when you redefine your life from the inside out. You will clear and clean up on the inside and outside, and you will automatically feel lighter. There is no need to harp on these changes. Believe me, in the greater scheme of things you will find that your attachments were of a lower vibration and you don't need them. There is no longer a need for them. They keep you third dimensional. And you are moving into being fifth dimensional beings. When you are a fifth dimensional being, you understand there is no need for attachment because you have the understanding that you can create all that you desire and, thus, don't find the need to attach to anything, as if it is going to go away. You will have a peace that you have never known as humans walking the earth. Can you imagine what that will be like? You will be one with the Universe at all times and will live in a state of what you would call magic, but is actually the natural state of the Universe. No longer will you feel need. Rather, you choose. Choose what you desire and then receive. There will no longer be the same obstacles to receiving your chosen desires because of the level of vibration you will be living in. So feel the joy of that understanding, and give thanks to God for all the gifts to be bestowed on you.

*   *   *   *

Here we stand at a critical moment in time. We have to choose love over fear. It's that simple. Those who choose love choose Light, and those who choose fear are really choosing darkness. What will you choose? What is your grandest purpose? Is it to live with chaos or God given gifts? Is it to nurture your fears or your grandest dreams? Only you can make this most vital choice. When you release your fears, you empower yourself and create a loving connection with your heart. Does that feel too "touchy feely" for you, to live from your heart? I tell you that there is no shame in living from your heart and to be in constant touch with your feelings, and, in fact, you will find a joy greater than you can imagine by living in this manner. To live from the heart, all things that come into your life will be seen via a heart connection first, not a mind connection. You will sense, feel, and honor everything in your world as a form of living energy. From that place, you will have a greater understanding of everything, which results in greater wisdom to guide you on your path. And all without getting your thinking part of you involved. Your heart has a wisdom that is greater than the mind. Your heart is the gateway to spiritual growth, not your mind. Feel your way into life. Feel your way into communicating with others. Feel your way into resolving conflicts. Feel your way into every part of your daily life. When you do this, you begin to see how much wisdom your heart holds. Trust it, like never before.

Channeling these words from Michael reminded me of a song called "Leading With Your Heart," sung by Barbra Streisand. I heard it many times more than a decade ago, and it left quite an impression on me. I knew it held great meaning, and I preserved the feelings the song imparted in my memory. I feel that living from the heart is the best way to live; however, it's such a challenge because the bulk of our society still values the "thinking self," more than the heart. Those of us who attempt to live from the heart are not always respected, and sometimes we're looked down upon as being weak and/or unwise.

Inspired by Michael's message, I searched out the actual lyrics and happily reunited with Barbra's beautiful ballad. As I read the lyrics, I paused with joy at the words, "Follow what you feel, feelings are wise." This is basically the same message that Michael just communicated. Yes, feelings *are* wise! When he stated those words about the wisdom of the heart, I thought how beautiful, and how true that is. However, we are not conditioned in our society to live this way. Obviously, that is changing. Humans will lead from their hearts in the Golden Age. Without being aware of it at the time, I realized that Michael had whispered to me to look up these lyrics to emphasize this very significant point.

Do not bother with living in the past. The past won't serve you and will only hold you back. There is no way you are ever going back to the way you once were. It is as if you are moving to a whole new planet, and on this planet you live differently. You think differently. You eat differently. You work, play, and just be in a whole different way. That's the new reality, and I implore you to shift your thoughts about your life and your world. Change is difficult for most humans, but when it is positive change, is it really so challenging? Think of it this way. You have this friend who you are used to being around your whole adult life. You are used to this friend, but this friend doesn't really support you, doesn't really care about you, and doesn't even have that much in common with you. But you are used to this friend. Being with this friend is really a habit. Along comes a new friend who meets all your desires of what a friend should be. Do you stick with the old friend, and spend your free time in this way because that is what you're used to? Or do you welcome this new friendship with open arms? Your old ways don't work anymore, and bless that! You are moving into higher vibrations that yield higher ways of being. Choose what serves you now and don't look back. Let go, accept, and adopt the new ways of being.

Oh, how Michael's words resonated with me. I am one of those who embrace change, for the most part. I love the newness of things, choosing all kinds of improvements, and being open to new possibilities in all aspects of my life. What I have found is that change is coming even easier for me, as well as for several people I know.

Many people are moving, changing their line of work, reviewing how they spend their time, and redefining their purpose and lives. (Of course, for those who have lost their homes and jobs, they are immediately thrust into new directions.) Once these seekers find their purpose, and redefine their life situations, the perfectly matched people come into their life as if by magic, and help them step into their new roles. The inner changes are astounding. They are meditating more, demanding more quiet time. They are simplifying their lives and lessening the overwhelming task of daily activities. They are clearing out the clutter, things they no longer need. They are learning to just be in the moment.

People are releasing their attachments to things, and the letting go process has become so much easier. This is part of the new energy. We can cope much better with change. We can simplify our lives and no longer be chained to our addictions. Most of us have some form of addiction. As Michael said, we can also ask our angels for help in letting go of them.

No one can tell you how to live your life. You have free will. However, if you want some advice, I will give it to you. Live peace, think peace, and fully be peace. When you adopt this way of intentionally being peace, you create it within your self and within your circles, which extends out into the world. Don't believe me? Tell me, when was the last time you had thoughts of peace. Were you able to maintain those feelings? Or did you say to yourself, "Oh, look, they're still sending more troops! They're now waging this war! There is still so much corruption!" How will this world ever have peace, you wonder, right? I tell you it will.

How are you maintaining peace in your own life? Or are you? Are you losing your temper for no good reason? Are you angry at your neighbor? Are you full of worry and fear? Find the peace within you, notice it and treasure it so that you are more conscious of these feelings. Treasure the peace within you and it will ripple outward. You feel each other's energies on very subtle levels. Your concentration on being peaceful within will be contagious. As that ripples out, the world changes. It starts with you.

*   *   *   *

Oh, Mary, I woke you up at 2:22 this morning and you weren't happy about it. But I did it for a reason, of course. You may not fully understand this, yet one day you will. The shifting energies of all of you on earth are causing you to recalibrate to the sun's energy. What does this really mean? It means, for one, that your cycles of sleep time are shifting. Many of you have woken up day after day in the "wee hours" such as around 2, 3, or 4 am for quite some time now. To sum it up, people are not going to need as much sleep as you have normally had in the past. You will "get by" on fewer hours. This will leave you with more time to manage your lives, and as you adjust, you will appreciate the extra hours to the day. To answer your question, yes, Liquid Light makes this possible. You won't need stimulants, such as caffeine, to get you through your day. With your bodies full of the most Divine Light energy, you will be stimulated naturally, and artificial stimulants will no longer be necessary or desired. And, yes, to answer this question of yours, the same goes for all recreational drugs including alcohol. The consumption of alcoholic beverages will no longer be desired. Can you imagine that the absence of these present-day vices for millions upon millions of people won't affect them? It's like a baby who moves on from strained food to food in a more solid form. He doesn't go back to his old routine of being spoon-fed mushy foods. He naturally moves on to independently eating solid foods, and is happy about it. This will be a natural process. You don't have to gorge yourself on these beverages now because you truly won't miss it, just like you don't miss strained foods! Please open your mind to accept this.

Okay, I knew this was coming, especially the news

about alcohol. Anything that speaks of lower vibrations cannot exist in the new energy, and that includes our beverages and foods that won't serve us anymore.

Yes, my dear, foods will change too. The dangerous additives, preservatives, antibiotics in meat, overdosing of sugar, and the list goes on and on, will no longer be tolerated by your bodies, or society itself. The truths about the poisoning of foods will continue to be revealed and corporations that proceed to manufacture and market dangerous foods will "fall." They need to change their ways, or they will fall. Do you realize the significance of the impact of these lowest of vibrational foods on your bodies? It is the main cause of disease, and no country remains untouched, although some are much more affected than others.

*   *   *   *

Life can seem to be so fragile, can't it? Scores of you are listening to your higher selves often without knowing it. And your higher selves are helping you to create your new reality for yourselves. As you go through this process, you can feel fragile and as if you aren't on sure ground. This is normal. It is as if you go through a period of unsettling, you recalibrate to the changes, and then the process happens again and again. But, oh, there is a rainbow on the other side of all these challenges, and you will feel the effects of it so profoundly that this reality you're presently in will be such a distant memory. Only you can make this journey. Only you can plow your way through to the new territory. But with your steadfastness and determination, we can help you through every mountain and valley, and we will be there to celebrate with you, a celebration unlike any ever in the Universe.

*   *   *   *

Today, I join Mary in a unique way as I speak to you. I am part of her physical body while she remains fully conscious. It is a melding of energies, so to speak. When we are together like this, I can speak so clearly to her mind. It makes her feel more confident when we are together in this way as she is presently working through her fears of putting this information out into the world. This is not an unusual occurrence. Angels often comfort humans who are in the midst of trying times and who need comfort. They aren't aware of what is happening, yet they suddenly feel better for no known reason. And so is the way for Mary right now. You can invite your angels to "meld" with you, to feel their energies. This was not possible until now for much of the unawakened population, since not only was this something too "out of the box" for them, but their vibrations weren't high enough for this to occur. For most of you, they are high enough now. Your angels wish for you to know this and to ask this of them, to help you feel the comfort from the angelic realms in a physical manner. As you get used to our energies, and as you continue to raise your own vibrations, the physical intensity of the "meldings," we'll call it, will increase. It's as if we are giving you little tastes of Heaven through the easiest way you can understand, on the physical level. When you request this, you must request with the solid intention that only the highest beings of Light are allowed to meld with you. Always voice this request. When you experience the melding the first few times, it may feel quite subtle. You may feel some tingling in your crown or your feet, and not much else. Other times you may feel a rush of energy flow through you. It may just take time to grow this melding

51

process. Be patient with it. Feel gratitude for it. Talk to your angels and listen to their words. Think of it as a most grand way to meditate. Yes, even the way you meditate is evolving. You'll be meditating alongside the angels, if you so choose. This will give you greater access and insight into the wisdom and peace the angelic realms have to offer you. So just flow with this process. You will be well pleased.

I was surprised by this message. Never would I have imagined telling others that angels would be merging with their bodies so that they could feel the comfort of Heaven. But the truth is, I can feel this merging. It is real. I feel tingly from head to toe and it is very loving, mystical, and calming—nothing to fear. If you really want to feel you are not alone, ask for a melding with your angel. To create Heaven on earth, this gift allows us to begin to feel what it will be like to become Light beings on earth.

Just find a quiet place, voice the request with the appropriate intentions as Archangel Michael described, and just allow. Try not to place expectations on the experience, but, rather, just be in the moment with it. I've noticed that when I go to sleep with the intention of experiencing a melding, I wake up with some recall of an even more intense experience than I have when I meld while awake, so I asked Archangel Michael why that is so.

The reason the melding seems more intense to you while you are sleeping, as you do have some memory of it when you awaken, is because in the sleep state, you are in closer access to your soul. So the melding involves the soul more directly than when you are fully conscious. I recommend just what you did when you took a nap today; request a melding just prior to your rest. You were in such a blissful state during your nap that you were telling your conscious self to remember it. Well, one day, as more of you practice the melding technique, and as you raise your

52

vibrations, the experience will be just as intense while awake.

When I experience the melding with Michael or my guardian angel, I sometimes feel this intense release going on deep in my head. It feels as if I am releasing all of my stress and heaviness there. This feels so good, better than the best head massage I could imagine, and it makes me feel so very calm and content afterwards.

If you are not comfortable with this practice, but wish to feel your angels' presence, you can just ask them to hold your hand or to hug you. In the past, when I experienced overwhelming difficulties, I asked God or Jesus to place me in an imaginary hammock as I curled up like a little girl, asking them to swing me back and forth, and I would see and feel this in my imagination. This may sound funny, yet it always helped me. Now, with the practice of melding, I feel the connection more directly, intensely, and is extremely comforting. Choose to connect with your angels in a way that is most comfortable for you.

*   *   *   *

Pop. Just like that. You are one of those who are giving away their past and setting yourself free. Just like that. Pop. You are already in a different life right now, yet in the same body. You don't have attachment to your past, to your memories, to anything. You are in the "Now," where you belong. This is where all of humanity who are choosing the Light, must and will experience. Suddenly, they get to a point and pop! The attachments are gone. It is so freeing, especially so when you consider what your new lives are going to be like. So let me give you a little preview right now.

Listen closely, for I do not want my words to be mis-

understood by readers. There will be Light both day and
night. Yes, you're hearing me right. There will be Light all
over your earth 24 hours a day. How can that be with the
planet revolving around the sun? Because there will be
spiritual Light filtered through you constantly. You will be
channeling golden Liquid Light through your beautiful
Light bodies. Do not be scared. If you believe that Heaven
will indeed be created on earth, wouldn't you expect to
carry bodies of Light, just as we do in Heaven? Wouldn't
you expect for everything to be quite different? Fear will
hold you back and will not serve you. I share this preview
so you can begin to understand what life will be like. As
you grow your acceptance, your transition will be so much
easier on your body, mind, and soul. Your acceptance will
broaden as you discern the information you're reading
here; and then the Universe will show you through
synchronicities, through dreams, and through your person-
al meditations, the validation you desire. Just ask.

Although I firmly believed this to be true, a beautiful validation came for me when I was previewing author Sherri Cortland's second book *Raising Our Vibrations for the New Age*[3] while in the editing stages of this book. She refers to the new Light in this way:

"Our sun is a source of 3rd dimensional light—we have plenty of that here already. The light we want to attract and hold is fifth dimensional light, and that light comes from the Great Central Sun... The Great Central Sun is the source for fifth dimensional energy and high-vibrational fifth dimensional light for our galaxy."

---

[3] Cortland, Sherri. *Raising Our Vibrations for the New Age*. Huntsville: Ozark Mountain Publishing, 2011.

And so I say, "Bring on the new Light." I intend to have as much as my physical being can hold at this point. Anyone else?

* * * *

How many of you really cherish your life? How many of you wake up every morning and feel gratitude for all you have? Nothing should be taken for granted. When you each bless all the miracles of your existence, you make room for more to be grateful for. Life isn't as grand when you aren't in appreciation mode. You can start living in that mode full time, right now. And when you find something that you are grateful for, take a moment to feel it in your heart. This action helps to open your heart. When you open your heart, you create a space to hold even more love, the love of God. God wants you to have what you desire. Your gratitude for every desire that manifests itself is actually felt by God. God connects with you through the heart. The heart connection allows God to maintain a direct relationship with you that is always present, but something that is your responsibility to nurture. It's like a plug in a socket that allows the energy to continuously flow, but if you don't turn on the lamp, it just sits there and there is no Light. So turn on the connection through feelings of gratitude. Through that action you can better feel God's love for you.

Love is the tonic that brings all who drink of it the greatest nourishment. For love feeds the soul greater than anything on your earth. Love is by no means something that can be accessed through need, but only by acceptance. Love is there for each and every one of you—from God, from your angels, from the earth body—and you need only allow it in. Many of you only seek love from your family and friends, but I tell you that the amount of love you receive from unseen sources is always unconditional and always present. You need to just allow and feel that love. Can you deny this love that is there for each of you? Can you at least imagine that there is this huge source of love for you that you're not consciously aware of? Get to know your angels. They will tell you and show you of their love for you. Your angels have been waiting for this time of your awakening to the love that is yours. They are also helping to connect you with you, meaning you with your soul. As you get to know your soul, you grow in self-love, and that's what many of you are moving towards. Knowing and loving you.

There is a window that most of you humans have kept shut lifetime after lifetime. It is the window to your soul. You have been disconnected from who you really are through your earthly incarnations. But, finally, at last, you will seek to open the window to reach your soul, find communion with your soul, and meld you with you. What happens when this opportunity is finally met? You live in a state of unconditional love for yourself and all around you. That is how we create peace on earth. As you all get in touch with your souls and live as who you really are—the eternal part of you, the part of you who resides in Heaven—peace reigns. There is no way it cannot be. Just as peace reigns in Heaven, you will create Heaven on earth when you become you.

While in the editing stages, I just re-read the above paragraph and felt something surging within me. I went into a fully ecstatic state, which came on unexpectedly. I surrendered to the experience of pure bliss traveling throughout my body. As the feelings subsided, I imagined what it will be like when we feel this internal bliss all the time, when we are in full connection with our souls. As I did so, the feelings of ecstasy fully returned.

You may ask, "How do you connect with your soul?" I tell you that it is through feelings of love. As you raise your vibrations while living in a state of love, you naturally get to know you—the real you. Because when you take the ego, the fears, and the negative emotions away, you uncover the pearl that is you. And it is a most glorious reunion; it is a blissful state. So intend to think, say, feel, and do all things from a state of love. When you wake up, be in that state of gratitude for what you have and the promise of the day before you, as gratitude itself is love. Work with your angels, talk to them, ask them for help if you so choose, because being in connection with them itself is love. Perform work and activities that fulfill you because fulfilling your purpose is love. Smile, laugh with, hug, and kiss those you love, and be kind to those you don't even know, because kindness is love. Infusing your day with love brings you closer to your soul. Focusing on what's wrong with the world, losing hope, taking life for granted, and feeling angry about everything maintains distance from your soul. The choice is yours. And when you go back to the old ways, you can choose again, and again, and again, until love becomes your way.

As I told Mary, who has heard the spiritual sound every day for the last fifteen years, the sound takes you closer to who you really are. She always notices it especially when she is thinking spiritually aligned thoughts, reading spiritual material, having a spiritual conversation, or while meditating. But she never really understood it. When you live in a state of love, you will notice this sound. Think of it as your lifeline to the Heavenly realms.

Yes, I hear this somewhat high-pitched sound in my

head on a daily basis, often throughout each day. I know there are many of you who experience it too, some who may not know that its source is spiritual, in nature. It has become a natural part of me, as natural as my own breathing. I never understood what to do with this gift, so I'm thankful to have this greater understanding, knowing that it is taking me closer to who I really am.

*   *   *   *

In every corner of the world is a mind-set. And they all differ. They all have their projections and beliefs about where your world is heading. Do not be swayed by others unless the information resonates with you. The best advice I can give all of you is to go within for your ultimate understanding. If you do not like or agree with the words on these pages, go within and listen to your inner voice. And if you ask the Universe to show you the truth, it will be shown to you. Don't get pulled into the fears and the negativity running rampant, whether it's coming from your coworker or friend, or from the news reports on the television. If you do "catch" that state of mind, just go within and find the peace and the truth. And do it again and again, if you have to. Your job as a human being on the planet at this time is by no means an easy one. Even though many of you have the luxuries and ease of modern day living, no lifetime has ever been nearly as challenging as this one. Watching your thoughts, words, feelings, and actions are critical. They represent your own mind-set. When you focus on love, instead of fear, you know you are on the right track. And do you know what happens when you focus on love? Your life improves, your days improve, your feelings improve, your relationships improve, and every thing improves. Outside of karmic retribution and the life challenges you chose prior to your incarnation, your life is reflective of your mind-set. So check in to your mind-set and see if it needs some tweaking or a total reset. If not, I congratulate you.

I think we can all agree that controlling our thoughts is one of the hardest things we can do. Even though I have improved my ability to control my thoughts, Michael also taught me something that works hand in hand with choosing to lessen negative thinking. He taught me to simply fill my life with love and kindness. When I choose to infuse love and kindness into every aspect of my life experience, these actions are filling my mind with positive thoughts. So I finally get it. When I concentrate on the "good stuff," it takes up lots of my thought time! And the more I do this, the less room there is to hold negative thoughts. It was a huge light bulb moment for me when I realized just how this can work so beautifully in one's favor!

Remember, not only is it a challenge to control our thoughts on a conscious level, our subconscious is reacting to all life situations and causing an effect, as well. For instance, if I had past lifetimes where I was manipulated by others, and I have not healed that in my subconscious in this life, whenever I find myself in situations where I'm being manipulated (because the Universe will keep on bringing manipulators into my life until I recognize the pattern and heal it), my thoughts can take over, creating such difficulty in trying to control them.

This is why it is so important to clear the past—in this life and our past lives—to heal from our struggles and pain that run us as if there were computer software in our subconscious minds. As you clear the past, it's easier to control your thoughts. I often ask my angels for help when I'm experiencing difficulty with this. It is truly extraordinary how they can help. Sometimes, it comes through the sudden kind words from a friend or even a stranger, which helps to quell the triggers of negative thinking. Again, focusing on love and gratitude is a sure-fire way to change our thoughts, words, feelings, and actions.

*   *   *   *

Bells and whistles. Many people like to have all the bells and whistles on their possessions; such as when you buy a car, you may prefer the extra gadgets that make driving more enjoyable and easier. Or on your washing machine so you have lots of choices to make when you gather your clothes and create the best wash possible.

Well, there are lots of bells and whistles to be enjoyed when you become the new human. Sound intriguing? Consider this. You will be able to read each other's thoughts. Yes, you will be telepathic. I can feel the fright many of you are feeling with that news. What if you think poorly of someone? Will they know your thoughts about them? How embarrassing that would be, right? And I can tell you that your thoughts will be different. No longer will ego drive you. The energy of love will drive you, and when you are in a state of love, and without fear, you think love-based thoughts. You want the best for everyone, and you no longer compete or find things to be jealous about. When you become telepathic, there is this ease and fluidity in communications. It is a compilation of thoughts driven by the heart, where your greatest wisdom lies.

Another change? Ease of movement. You will no longer have the weight of your physical bodies to hinder your ability to move freely and easily. As Light bodies at some future point in time, you will be able to get from place to place with just a mere thought. Can you imagine that?

That is how we get around here. When you call upon me, your thought brings me to you instantaneously. Some of you more adventurous types are thrilled by this news. Others are scared. But I tell you, who you really are is one who moves in this way. When you "die" or, as more appropriately described, "transition," this is how you move, so you will eventually move in this way while being on earth. This is what Heaven on earth is, and I will continue to remind you to help you wrap your mind around this.

When you transition fully into light bodies, your DNA changes and your bodies' directives in how it functions all shift instantaneously. No longer will your weight slow you down. You will be fluid in all ways. You will move in Light. You will create opportunities unlike that a human has ever experienced. For instance, you will one day be able to fly, levitate, or move suddenly and within the moment of a single thought.

"Okay, I feel you just lost nearly this whole reading audience on this one. I am thirsty for understanding all that the Golden Age will bring, but I feel like I'm channeling science fiction."

Your concerns are understood. After all, many readers, as I can see them in what is your future time, are agreeing that this sounds like science fiction. Yet, these are abilities that will be inherited in the Golden Age.

"Then why am I not seeing this everywhere else, from all the other channelers regarding the new age? I have to be hearing you incorrectly."

There are several others who have channeled this information, but many are unable to put this out there for fear of being wrong or fear of being ridiculed. Again, I say that if you believe that you are creating Heaven on earth, is this not conceivable?

"So there will be no need for airplanes?"

Air travel, boat travel, train travel, and all other means to move from one place to another will eventually cease to exist. You will move as spiritual beings first, not physical beings. Your spiritual gifts are what will be the "gas" driving you to your destinations. You do not need to understand just how all this can possibly happen, but rather celebrate the gifts that you will assume.

Once again, I received validation from the Universe during the editing process of this book, and, again, while previewing Sherri Cortland's *Raising Our Vibrations for the New Age.* She channels her guide Gilbert who explains:

There will be vehicles although they are not really needed, but the first wave will want them because they will feel familiar, yet as life goes on over time there will be less of that kind of thing because all will be able to simply think themselves where they want to be. Because there will be no need to have oil or gasoline to power vehicles, they will be powered through telekinesis, and there will be no reason for countries to fight over what used to be considered valuable resources.

Michael continued:

It is your mind that will have difficulty for most of you to accept the new ways; however, your heart will lead the way if you allow it to. Do you know why? Because your heart is so tired of the way things are and have been. You are sick of war, sick of hatred, sick of greed, sick of corrupt ways, sick of poverty, sick of the mistreatment of humans, animals, and the earth herself, sick of games, sick of callousness, sick of pettiness, sick of the shallowness, sick

*of the "dog-eat-dog" mentality, and the list goes on and on.
You are ready for a better way of living, and your heart
wants it. Your souls, as a collective, signed up for it. Your
ego, your brain, and your set-in-your-ways-and-don't-like-
change parts of you may fight it. Again, I ask you to ask
your angels and Archangels for help in your acceptance.*

*There is another change that you will surely welcome
once you experience it, and that is Liquid Light. Having
Light pouring through your body is nothing new, for those
of you who meditate often consciously use Light to do so.
Yet Liquid Light is different. Liquid Light also comes
directly from God and it fills you with all you need to
sustain you. I'm firmly aware that this may sound like
science fiction to you as well, but only ask that you request
to receive the Liquid Light. Ask for a sampling of it
because your level of vibration may not be high enough to
receive much of it, and then decide for yourself. You can
feel a portion of the effects so as not to overwhelm your
body. Yet, there will come a day when you will channel it
fully, naturally, and it will be a constant supply.*

*With the full transmission of Liquid Light once you
shift into the fifth dimension, your bodily needs, eventually, will no longer exist. At some future point in time,
you will no longer need food or water to sustain you. At
some future point in time, you will no longer need to
exercise in order to maintain your health. Liquid Light
will give you all you need. I realize that this is hard for
many of you to believe.*

*So much of what you feel about these concepts and
properties of your new way of living is out of fear. If you
just look at Liquid Light as the life-giving substance that
all beings in Heaven live off of, and you are creating the
dimension of Heaven on your earth, is it something to fear?
I ask you to consider this most important question? Would*

you rather continue to live on a planet that is overwhelmed with violence, tyranny, oppression, and disrespect of human, animal, and earthly life? Or would you rather choose to live on a planet filled with love and Light? Once you feel the effects of Liquid Light, your fears will melt away because you will feel the ecstasy of Heaven, and you will not want to be without.

"Will we still be able to touch each other, as Light beings?"

Yes. You will be able to touch and be touched. Except that the touches will be more deeply felt, as the energies of that exchange of touch will be powerful.

"Will we still have sexual relations as Light beings?"

This is one aspect of living in the new earth that will be hard to completely understand. Sex as you experience it as a physical person will not be the same. It will be a much grander experience. The intensity of the union of souls as Light beings is such that your minds would have difficulty understanding. As it is for many of you now, the physical enjoyment of sex is hard to surpass. Most of you find it to be your greatest physical feeling you can experience while on earth. But I tell you that as Light beings, when you commune with another soul, it creates an ecstasy greater than what you know now. And I know what I say next will create much discomfort for some. The communing of souls will no longer be concerned with the distinction of male with female, male with male, or female with female. It will be being with being, soul with soul. The labels and distinctions will fall away.

*　　　*　　　*　　　*

Let me make clear that there are some people who need to make choices that are not easy ones. They fulfilled their contracts on earth, but don't want to leave. They have that freedom to stay, and they can change their contract. What I'm saying is, if someone's "time has come," yet they wish to remain on earth for the shift, they can do so. Or they can reincarnate and start the cycle again. So many have left the planet in recent years. For some, it was too hard for them to cope with all the energy shifts and changes, and seeing the planet in such chaos, and they gladly accepted the ends of their contracts. But there are those whose contracts were about to end, yet they didn't want to leave, and they do have that choice on a soul level.

Is it not true that you chose this lifetime to be in? When you remain aware of that, it somehow makes the difficulties easier to cope with. You are already reaping many of the rewards that are coming into play as the veil between Heaven and earth has thinned so much now. Magic and miracles have become part of your daily life, and they help you deal with the challenges you're experiencing now. Depending on how much soul work you have done, whether clearing, releasing, and/or refining, many of you are finding the intensity of your challenges reduce significantly. And that is the reward for doing your work.

When difficulties arise, often one on top of another and on top of another, they are showing you there is something you need to acknowledge, clear, and let go of. If the situations are forcing you to stand up for yourself, for example, choose to stand up for yourself and get the lesson now. If you keep finding yourself in relationships that make you cower, this is telling you something. End the pattern by the correct action. Once you get it and learn the lesson, your challenges will lessen.

I understand it is not easy. When you're going through the difficulties you want to cry and scream, and may do so. But you eventually come to a place of understanding that these experiences helped you grow, and you learn to bless the difficulties. This is not easy, but when you get to this place it is so comforting to just be thankful for the growth that would not have come without those lessons that taught you.

The harder part is when you have to forgive and stop holding grudges toward others. Those people who were mean to you or hurt you or disgraced you also helped you help yourself. And forgiveness is always necessary. Your inability to forgive hurts you much more than the other person. Forgiveness equals freedom. Forgiveness busts your heart wide open to receive love from others. Lack of forgiveness keeps your heart closed and can lead to depression and self-inflicted emotional replays that wound the soul. Forgive and move on.

*   *   *   *

Do you know that I can be in millions of places at once? I know that is hard to believe or understand, but you can call on me, Archangel Michael, right now and I'll be with you. My attention won't be diverted because I am with so many others at the same time. I am with you completely. Ask me to hold your hand and I will hold it. Do you feel me holding your hand right now? Because I am holding your hand. And this is the way it is with all angels and Archangels. You can call on any of us and we are here for you. We hope you will choose to have a conscious relationship with us so we can help you.

There is an angel who is with you all the time. This angel is assigned to you and only you. You also have other angels and guides that come and go according to what is going on in your life and who can best serve you, but this one angel, your guardian angel, always remains. I ask you to connect with your angel. Talk to your angel every day and build that relationship. This has always served immeasurable benefits, but now it proves to be even more valuable. Your angels can see things you cannot. They can guide you through these challenging times. They can help you with your relationships. They can help you turn the corner on some change in your life. They can especially provide the support you need to get through to the other side as this planet evolves. So talk to your angels and ask them for help. Feel their comfort through "melding," or to hold your hand, as they will always show their presence.

Until you become aware of them and call on them, your angels' relationships with you are very one-sided. None of us can interfere in your lives unless you ask because you have free will. Once you ask, the possibilities of the ways we can help you would astound you. Give it a try if you wish. Your angel wants nothing more than to help you, but you have to make the first step—so just ask.

When the help comes from a stranger's words or a call from a friend or an opportunity that comes from out of the blue, you are apt to give that stranger, friend, or situation behind the opportunity the credit, as that is human nature. It's hard to get your heads around the fact that angels are actually often behind it. They are whispering things to you all the time, and they can whisper words to say, things to take action on, whatever helps you as long as it is in your highest interest. When your intentions are pure and honest, and you desire what's in your highest interest, you will receive the help you desire.

*   *   *   *

Love should be the focus of your every day. Are your words coming from a place of love? Your thoughts? Your feelings? How about your actions? When you embrace the emotion of love, you cannot help but attract more love into your life, and you cannot help but have an effect on the planet as a whole. Yes, just one person does make a difference. Every act, feeling, thought, and word that involves love raises the individual's vibration as well as the planet's vibration. Your focus on love attracts other love-centered people. Have you noticed more love-centered people in your life? They are very enjoyable to be around. The effects are contagious.

If you want to attract more love-centered relationships, stop being so concerned about every action or word that comes from others. Stop reacting to everything as if you have full understanding of what is going on with the other person, because you do not. Rather, just be and enjoy what is presented to you in any given moment with not judgment, but joy, and with not lack, but rather abundance. Accept that which others can provide and don't expect more. Only be concerned about who and how you want to be, and not concerned whether someone is meeting your expectations or not. This is hard for most of you. Humans can be fragile and can experience unnecessary hardship over and over again.

Do you know what love really is? It is an emotion, and it is one that is grounded in Light. Love is Light and it comes directly from Source. Every time you feel love, or are in a state of love, you are connecting to God's energy. It is in this state of love that you uncover all the untruths, misunderstandings, lies, misbeliefs, et cetera, and see what is truly there—love. For love is all there really is. People just take love energy and distort, manipulate, redefine, and change the energy to something that no longer looks like love, until you unravel it to find its true essence. So that means if you hate thy neighbor, but then release the arguments, the words, the misunderstandings, the anger, the misbehavior, and look at him, you see that at his core essence is love. If you hate another, but then start to see they come from God as you do, well that does not mean that you have to join them for tea; but you can forgive and let go, and take notice of the love at their very core. The world isn't as scary a place when you see that at its core all comes from love.

It is commonplace for people to look for love as they move through each day. Who will love me? Who will appreciate me? Who will notice me? Who will comfort me? Humans feel they need to constantly seek it outside of themselves, but I tell you it is within. You are love itself, and you don't need your daily dose of outside reminders of who you are. You already are. So instead of basing the success of each day by how much love you received from the outside, I ask you to begin to find it within. When you find the love within you, and love yourself for the beautiful being that you are, you will attract reflections of that love from others. It cannot not be so! The Law of Attraction will bring you reflections of your self-love, which includes your love of God. Embrace that relationship and just see who walks into your life. Everything, everything starts from within. If you want love and all the by-products of love, which include joy and peace—then live from the inside out, rather than the outside in.

Life as you know it will change when make this simple switch. Yes, I say simple because your nature may be to label this difficult. Start your day in a state of gratitude for yourself and your life. Watch your self-talk and make sure you are treating your own self with love, respect, and honor. Take care of yourself, not just others, and move yourself up on the ladder of your priorities. Be as concerned about the way you talk about yourself in your mind, as you are concerned about how you come across to others. Are your self-thoughts coming from love or self-disgust? Are they forgiving or chiding? When you tune in, recognize, and make any necessary changes, they will change what and whom you attract into your life.

Do you want to know another simple switch? Take yourself on vacation. You don't have to go on a plane or in a car for this; you can take a vacation right in your own home. Turn off the television, the phone, the computer, and all other distractions, and find a place of quiet and ask for God to shower you with His love. Imagine God's love filtering through your whole being. Let him take away your pains, frustrations, exhaustion, and problems, and replace it all with love. Love will cleanse you from all you want a vacation from. Let his Light fill you to overflowing, and show love for yourself as you are filled with love knowing you are deserving of it. And when you are done, feel gratitude for God and His love, as well as for yourself. This is a vacation you may take anytime you wish.

* * * *

Life as you know it will no longer be. What did you feel when I just spoke these words to you? Fear? Excitement? Not sure? These words are not meant to frighten you, but I cannot control your reaction, only you can. What I can do is offer you a picture of what your daily life will be like as we create Heaven on earth, and then you decide how you feel about this.

First of all, the ways of the world have not been "working." The planet would have headed right into total destruction had you, as a collective, allowed it to. But your souls collectively chose a different route and that's what I wish to describe to you.

Bliss. That is the word that best describes what your new lives will be—just bliss. You will all recognize each other, but your love for each other will have grown because you will see each other as whom you really are. Your souls will shine through your general appearance. You will be more youthful and glowing, and you will be in bliss.

Life will appear the same at first glance. You still have the trees, the buildings, the homes, the land, and many of the things that you are used to seeing. However, upon closer look, nothing is really the same, because every single thing will have raised its vibration. Every rock, every tree, every person, every animal, every thing will be of a higher vibration. What does this mean? It means that what moves into the fifth dimension, this Heavenly created earth, belongs there. If it's not there, it either chose not to be there, or could not possibly exist in a higher dimension.

You will not be sad about what is no longer there or the old life on earth you left behind. Your feelings of bliss within will not allow you to. Rather, you will celebrate the saving of your beloved planet and the promise of the best humanity has ever revealed of itself, its very souls. When you become who you really are, and live more from your souls rather than your personalities, you feel bliss and you would not want it any other way. You see, the soul is rich and multifaceted. You will learn so much about you, and you will love you. You will love others. And when you live from the heart, from the place of love, there lies the core of your bliss.

It is easy to think negatively about yourself in the third dimension because you don't yet know who you really are. But those negative self-thoughts won't exist when you shift. You won't look at your body and be disgusted or frustrated about the imperfections. You won't be looking at your spouse or friend and wanting to change them anymore.

You won't be angry at society for all the ways it has disappointed you. You will be in love with you, with love itself, and you will see everything around you with new eyes.

Can you imagine that? Many of you are already starting to have these new feelings, this new way of seeing. You know that we are moving in this direction as a collective. It is a natural progression. You may not know exactly when it started or how it happened, but the fact is, you shifted from living from your mental state toward living from your heart state. This is the way to live and see differently—from the heart. It is the only way.

As a new human, you won't be missing the old self. It will be as if you reincarnated without having to "die." You will look at this life as a past life and will celebrate the transition you made. You will celebrate your ability to transition, but you won't miss the old self or the life you had. There will be new opportunities beyond your imaginings right now, and you will embrace them and the joy and growth they will bring.

Right now, take a look at who you spend your time with and what you spend your time doing. Many of you have taken notice of the many relationships that have just changed or no longer exist. Your daily activities are changing as well. It's as if you are re-prioritizing everything in your life and making new choices. This has been a natural process. When you hone in on your purpose, you find that the Universe brings to you, as if by magic, just who can help and support you in your work, as well as in friendship. You marvel at whom you meet and how you meet them. There are no coincidences here.

And speaking of coincidences, there are actually no coincidences, period. Some people don't want to believe that what is known as coincidence indeed carries meaning, often because it scares them. That makes the world too magical, and humans want to make sense of everything. And I say to you, get used to the magic. It's going to continue to increase. Synchronicities are on the rise. Miracles are on the rise. And when you desire and celebrate them, you attract more. This channel is, you might say, obsessed with them, and she also attracts splendid signs and what she considers to be magical moments every single day.

I wrote my first book *I Can See Clearly Now: How Synchronicity Illuminates Our Lives* to further open peoples' minds to the magic and miracles our Universe provides. What I found absolutely stunning was the number of readers who shared with me synchronicities that were spin-offs of the very ones I shared in the book.

For instance, I wrote about my incredible string of synchronicities involving chihuahuas. One reader wrote me that as soon as she started reading the book, a chihuahua was suddenly hanging out at the end of her driveway, a dog she had never seen in her neighborhood before. I also described my experiences of seeing the number combination 444, which is a special sign from the angels—and readers would see it constantly or even wake up at 4:44, just as I mention in the book. In fact, a reader told her mother, who also read the book, to look for 444s as they were driving. Just after she said that, she saw my last name, "Soliel," right there on a building.

I believe these things happened, often with the help of the angels, and in addition to the magic of the Universe, to prove to these readers that the phenomenon of synchronicity is real. Society has discouraged the noticing of signs, or meaningful coincidences, but that seems to be changing as we evolve.

It will be impossible to not notice the magic of the Universe. There will be a profound intensity of miraculous occurrences experienced by each of you, such that the way in which you each see the world, the Universe, will intensely change in a multitude of ways. It will be glorious.

*   *   *   *

Love is the answer. When you don't know if you should trust, if you should leave, if you should give, if you should believe—love is always the answer. As you live from your heart, you will always know what to do, how to act, or which way to go.

Say someone calls you on the phone, you think it's a sales call, and so then you let the answering machine pick it up. Then something makes you just pick it up yourself and the person on the other end speaks to you with such kindness. It was indeed a sales call, and it's regarding a product or service you are not interested in, but that kindness extended between you makes you both feel good. In fact, it puts you in a much better mood, as if you had someone smiling right through the phone, and your mood changes for the day.

Perhaps you had a tiring afternoon and come home to your family, and your little toddler is pulling on your trousers wanting you to play with him the moment you walk in the door. You have your eye on the couch and television, but just when you're about to say, "Not now," you have a change of heart and scoop up that boy. And in what seems an instant, you suddenly don't feel tired but rather energized.

Love and kindness are what sustain you now. You seek them out constantly, ever so constantly. You are magnets to love and kindness now, and you don't want to stand for anything other than those feelings that feed the soul. You want to be easier on each other; your desire to fight, complain, and argue are diminishing as you surrender to *love, and want love to show itself everywhere. And that very wish of yours will become the new reality.*

The familiar adage, "Do onto others as you would have them do onto you," has always been a true and revealing statement; because how you treat others, you reap the same in return. If you treat others with respect, you will be respected. If you lie to others, you will be lied to. If you express kindness to others, you will be treated with kindness yourself. This is the way it has always been. But how do you think this will evolve?

As you raise your vibrations, you cannot help but treat others well, better than you ever have. Even when someone upsets you, instead of striking out and not treating him or her well, you feel compassion and soften your behavior. Anger no longer dwells in the heart, but rather love does. Bitter and hurtful words no longer spew outward, but rather words of kindness and understanding and support.

It's not because you suddenly become fragile and you just let people step over you. No. You see each other as who you really are, which is love. And love deserves love in return. There is no reason to compete with, indignify, or destroy another, but rather to only love and honor one another. When we speak of peace on earth, we talk not just of the cessation of wars, but the peace between everyone. The peace starts with you recognizing your soul, and then the souls of others. Once you remember who you really are, peace reigns.

Does that sound too good to be true? In Heaven, we work and live in cooperation with each other. We don't yell or argue; those actions are not part of us. There is no need or desire for it, and this shall be the same for you. You will not need or desire to hurt another in this new earth. Your only desire will be to love, and just be love.

When it is time to go to bed, what are your thoughts

about? Are you just happy to lay your body down and think about the rest you are looking forward to? Are you thinking about the day you just experienced? Are you thinking about your worries or concerns about the future? Going to sleep can hold much excitement for you, as there are wonderful experiences to behold during your sleep times.

Imagine traveling to another place in your sleep. Your spirit can travel. It always has been able to, without your being aware, most likely. But what if you start becoming aware? What if you consciously choose to travel? On any given night, you can ask your guardian angel to accompany you and go wherever you wish. As beings in Heaven, we travel by thought. We think where we want to go and we are there. When you create Heaven on earth, you will be eventually able to do the same, but it will start by doing so in your sleep.

As you raise your vibrations, you will begin to soul travel, consciously, and some of you already are experiencing this. If this is something you desire, tell your angels you wish to travel and for them to accompany you, and when the time is right, you will know it. Again, many of you may find this scary, but it is only because the concept may be new to you. Every one of you has soul traveled, yet most of you have remained unaware. There is so much for you to be made aware of now that the veil between Heaven and earth has thinned.

Which brings me to my next wish for you. I wish for you to request for your angel's presence and allow them to touch you to prove to you of their existence. They can hold your hand and you can feel the tingling of energy there. They can move your head very gently. Angels love to give feet washings, especially when you've had a difficult day. These are energetic and you can actually feel your feet being "washed," and it is most comforting. This channel often experiences feet washings and especially appreciates it when she forgets she is not alone when going through a life difficulty. She often wakes up with her feet being washed.

This very morning I woke up in this way, in fact. Knowing my angels are with me, and having that reminder that they love me, helps me face the day no matter what challenges or obstacles I may encounter. I cannot imagine a better way to start my day than with this gift from the angels.

When you allow yourself to feel these sensations, it is not something you can explain away. Your whole concept of reality changes as you really open yourself up to the unseen, and the gifts coming from the unseen.

As I reread words that I channel, I become concerned about readers' reactions to them. I know these words may scare some but, again, so much of what we are scared of is that which we don't really understand. And that's usually because it is unknown and has not yet been experienced. This is very new information for many of us. But when you consider that Heaven is our true home, and as we bring more of our true home into our lives, we become more of who we really are. So there really is nothing to fear. We are just connecting to home and receiving the glories of Heaven without having to "die."

Before us all is our greatest opportunity for adventure. Many people love to witness others experiencing various adventures, but this is our chance to actually live the greatest adventure of all our incarnations, that we are each an active part of.

For those of you who disbelieve much of what is being said in this volume, I suggest you at least give this guidance a chance. Whatever is going to happen is going to happen. Would you not rather be prepared just in case this material is accurate? Would you rather not know of the tools and assistance you have within you and around you? There are millions upon millions of people who are fully aware that something is up, that you are at the precipice of great change. This is not the time to close your heart to others or close your awareness to information and understanding that will help you. The earth needs you to help usher in the new age of humanity.

Why is it that people can be so hardened to change? They resist change more than they resist anything else. One reason is the belief that change is work, but what if change is relief? Another reason is that the "same 'ol, same 'ol" is familiar, and they want what is familiar and what they can count on. I can understand that it is a feeling of great comfort to keep things the same, yet stagnation doesn't allow one to grow. And the fact is, there is nothing more familiar to who you really are than Heaven itself. You must start seeing things with new eyes realizing and accepting the changes that are occurring and will continue to occur, and start learning to embrace the adventure. You always have the choice, the free will to stay just where you are, and choose to remain behind.

*   *   *   *

Many of you feel you are stuck in difficult situations with friends and family. For some, they don't understand all your "new age" talk and think you're not all there in the mind. Some are actually mad at you for you have distanced yourselves from the religion you were brought up with. In these situations, you can just be. Be the love, be the Light, be the calm, be the peaceful, and be the example in all ways. Hopefully, your Light will become contagious, but you cannot change another or make someone under-

stand, even when he or she is a member of your family.

There are growing numbers of people who see the Light, and you can seek them out. Find ways to communicate. Be in touch on a regular basis so that you can provide each other support. As important as it is to gather, your most important and necessary work will be done within you.

And so now, I wish to remind you that you ultimately "Be Love." Commit to being love at all times. Be in love with you. Are you appreciating and loving yourself every day? The ascension process is difficult. Those of you who are making great strides are not appreciating your own efforts. You must take time to feel the love for yourself, as well as others. Work with your angels. To go through this process without your angels is like ignoring the best Christmas gift you have ever received. You have free will and can choose to go it alone. It is your choice. Lighten your mind. Follow your heart! Become a representative of peace.

Notice I did ask you to stop hating, but rather to be love. I did not ask you to end war, but to be peace. Focus on the desired reality you wish! Do not focus on the way it is and try to change it—you will get "trying to change it." Just be what you wish to be: love, peace, and one that lives from the heart. You cannot go wrong when you focus on this way of being.

Can you imagine what it would be like if you were left alone and ignored? It would not be fun. That is what it is like for your angels when you ignore them. They are left with a job they are so willing and excited to perform, but without you recognizing them or working with them, they can only watch you as you stumble and strain and miss out on all the gifts that could be bestowed on you. No one could be more on your side than your angel. They want *what is best for you. How refreshing is it that there is no competition in this relationship? They love you without condition. Even when you ignore them or close your mind to their existence, they love you so much. They know how to help you meet the goals you signed up for in this life. But most often they just wait. They show you signs all the time telling you, "I'm here for you and I love you." Yet even the signs often go unnoticed. They cannot interfere beyond that so they wait, and wait.*

If you want to start taking notice of your angels, start by thanking them for what they do for you. Thank your guardian angel, who is with you all the time, and those angels and guides that come and go according to your needs and the phases of your life. After you show them loving gratitude, start to talk to them every day. Get into the practice of asking them for help.

When you have a problem or frustration, just talk to them as you would talk to your friend, and ask them for their help. Sometimes, you will be blessed with a miracle, and, sometimes, you will receive some form of help, but you need to do your part too. Think of your angel as a coworker who has amazing abilities, who is like a magician that can make unearthly things happen, and who can whisper thoughts to people and give them wonderful ideas. Think of your angel in that way, because as you are working alongside them, you have celestial help that cannot compare with any kind of help available on your earth. Get into this habit and you will see the miracles increase in your life.

I ask you to not carry expectation of how the angels will help you, just know they will. Now this is very important for you to understand: they always hear you and they always support you. However, if you feel they aren't helping you, as this or that problem just isn't going away, it might be because it is your lesson, a lesson that must be learned so that you can move on and don't have to revisit it ever again. Know they are still assisting you, but are nudging you to work through the lesson.

This is a hard thing for humans to understand. When they finally do develop relationships with their angels, they come to a point where they think it was futile. They think it was all in their minds that the angels were helping, but if you could only see what's going on here. Your angels are supporting you. They are helping and loving you beyond what you can imagine. But their help may be one of support and nurturing and advising at times because they cannot do your lessons for you. They help you "get it." They help you understand the lesson, yet it is your lesson. Don't ever, ever give up on your angels!

It's nice to have angel statues and gadgets and things outside and around you that remind you of the angels in your life. It also makes your angels happy. But do this while focusing on the real angels that are there for you. Focus on them every day. Just as you can be in the habit of calling your mother or your friend every day, you can "call" your angels. A problem—call. A desire—call. Sad or lonely—call. Scared—most definitely call. Call on me. I will always protect you and I can be in many places at one time. No call is unimportant. Call on me, Archangel Michael. Call on any Archangel. If you don't know whom to call on, ask your guardian angel to call on who can best help you.

Some of our children get this. When you tell them that their angels are always watching over them, and they can talk to their angels, they will more than likely agree or already know all about it. Angels more easily become part of their everyday conversation. When they talk about a problem, they may tell you not to worry because their angels are helping them. Children are so beautifully open. They can actually help to get us in the habit of talking to our own angels.

When you see a friend in trouble and you wish to help, would you suggest they ask their angels for help? This is what I've finally learned to do. I don't care what the friend thinks of my idea. I step out of my comfort zone and talk about things that aren't normally talked about. And then something amazing and, often, unexpected can happen; they say something like, "I hadn't thought to do that. Thanks!"

We can do this for each other. We can remind each other of our angels' existence. I know I still need reminders to remember to ask. My goal is to get to the point where as soon as I need help or direction, my first thought goes to my angels: "Please help me." Sometimes it does, but not always. If not, I'll usually get a sign reminding me of their presence. This is all about habit. As we learn to share our lives with our angels on a conscious basis, it becomes effortless, and the rewards are phenomenal.

Angels do not want to be glorified or worshipped; they only want to help us, support us, and love us. Many believe that we should only be asking God, Jesus, Mother Mary, Buddha, or whatever Deity corresponds to our religious beliefs for help. However, I feel that God did not give us angels to watch over us just to see what we're up to every day. It is an important part of our spiritual growth to become aware of all the Divine presences in our lives, and to honor God's gifts to us by acknowledging them, and calling on them for assistance and advice. In my view, we are honoring God best by noticing, accepting, and utilizing the multitude of gifts we are graced with.

One more point about being open with our friends and loved ones regarding our angels or any topic that has a "new age" slant on it. We cannot change this world for the better without stepping outside of our comfort zones, and we should halt the worrying about what others think of us. I tell myself this often so that I have the courage to speak the words, the truth, of what Archangel Michael as well as my heart are guiding me to say. We must go outside the box in our thoughts, words, feelings, and actions. Staying inside the box is not working for this world. Breaking free and embracing a new way of living will also keep us from being closed off and living in fear.

I tell you, we are entering this new age. This reality is already set, but your place in it is yet to be determined. We know the work is not easy, yet one day, if you aren't yet aware, you will firmly understand that you chose to do this work. You, your soul, chose to be here at this momentous time. And as you connect more and more with your soul, you better understand your path to this new age. With all your challenges and difficulties, you are also being showered with magic and miracles on a daily basis. Are you recognizing them? For instance, did you know that the rainbow in the sky was for you? Did you know that the compliment that came from "out of the blue" was a message from your angels delivered through a human? Did you know that your healing was a Divine intervention? Did you know you were held all night in the loving arms of your angel? I ask you to start taking notice of your gifts, and celebrate and appreciate them with your heart.

One reason this book was written was to bring awareness to the amazing resources we all have to tap into. In fact, nothing brings me as much joy as recognizing the gifts of our angels and the Universe. They greatly soften the difficulties I go through as I constantly adjust through the shifts that we are all experiencing. They are like kisses on my cheek that say "I love you," and "You are worthy," and I celebrate each one immensely. People may think I overreact or wonder why I get so excited time and time again. Yet, I believe we owe it to our angels to be excited and happy about their gifts. And these feelings of gratitude only bring forth more to be grateful for.

*   *   *   *

It is an illusion to believe that things will stay the same. I think all of you who found your way to this book really don't want things to stay the same. Yet, at the same time, you are also fighting change. But I tell you, you must embrace change and you must make the changes within you. There is no way out of this. However, with the techniques I am sharing in these messages, you can make it much easier on yourself by recognizing and working with your angels, most especially.

I will tell you about another technique that will help you immensely. Breathe consciously. Some of you sighed to yourself when I said that. You may think of the many times authors, healers, and workshop leaders told you to put your awareness on your breath, but, perhaps, you never experienced the spiritual, emotional, or physical gain it created. I tell you that breath opens the door to gifts beyond your imaginings. And now like never before. So give this a chance.

Right now, focus on your breath. As you breathe in slowly and fully, imagine breathing in ecstasy, whatever that means to you. If you are not sure what it would feel like, just use your imagination of what ecstasy would feel like. Yes, and then breathe out, but getting ready to breathe in more ecstasy. As you begin to feel ecstatic feelings through your being, expect more as you breathe in again and again, and let the feelings build. Imagine you are breathing in a taste of Heaven. Know that you are allowing God's love to fill you and let the feelings flood you completely—every cell of your body and every aspect of your being. Let it take over and just keep allowing the feelings of ecstasy to run through you.

Now, the next time you have feelings of upset or frustration, or when you are fighting change in your life, breathe in the taste of Heaven. As you do, remember what all of your present difficulties are moving you toward; they are moving you toward the ecstasy. When you breathe in and think ecstasy on each breath, build deeper and deeper into these feelings. Let them wash over your temporary difficulties; wash them right out of your mind and just be with ecstasy.

Some of you may feel uncomfortable with the word or feeling of ecstasy. It may sound sexual in nature, and it surprises you that this Archangel would ask you to call this forth. And I tell you that sexual energy experienced as humans is similar to the energy that is felt by us in Heaven. The bliss we feel in Heaven is similar in nature to the bliss you feel when engaged in sexual relations; however, these feelings don't originate in sexual organs. In Heaven, we feel this bliss throughout our beings as if we are being constantly washed in blissfulness. As you continue to experience tastes of Heaven, you will understand what I speak of.

If you don't feel ecstasy the first time you try this technique, do not give up. Try again, and over time, and with complete focus on the breath, you will be increasingly rewarded for your efforts. This is really a meditation, and, of course, all meditation is good for us and brings forth feelings of peace and often enlightening information. It helps to close the eyes to better connect with your feelings while experiencing this breathing technique. And remember, as you would after any meditation, to always ground yourself following the experience. Just like learning to drive a car, it takes practice to learn to meditate, to remember to ask your angels for help, and to learn and become comfortable with the techniques given throughout this book.

Many people who experience near-death experiences (NDEs) do not want to return to earth having experienced the ecstasy of Heaven. While I have often felt these feelings of ecstasy when practicing this technique, on a few occasions, I actually pushed the feelings aside because it was so intense that I felt I couldn't contain it or could lose consciousness. But as soon as I pushed it away, I immediately found myself wanting it to return. Sometimes, the feelings come spontaneously without even initiating the technique. One day, this will be our constant and natural state of being.

*   *   *   *

As you continue to spread Light, the last of the darkness on your planet leaves. There has been so much darkness. Not just about what you read in your newspapers or watch on the television, but there is darkness of such great magnitude that is very little known, and yet it is becoming slowly revealed. Because of the Lightworkers spreading the Light, these dark forces are dismantling on their own. I tell you that where there is Light, darkness cannot remain. There will be shocking and upsetting news of the darkness that has resided among all of you. And many of you will be glad you never knew about it as it would have been too hard to bear knowing about. It would have ripped at your sense of well-being. But know that this battle is almost over. Always think, feel, speak, and act with love and Light. This is your protector. Love and Light will never fail you.

As news of the darkness continues to get revealed, do not let this affect your Light. Celebrate that the Light has exposed it, knowing that it will and must come down. Celebrate these final falls of that which does not serve humanity and have actually imprisoned humanity for so long. Understand and revel in the power of the Light, and don't look back. Revel in the win, and don't put your thoughts and energies on the fallen darkness. There is no time to dwell on it, but rather, stay focused on the next steps humanity must take to move into a Golden Age.

*   *   *   *

No matter what part of the world you are from, you are all feeling the effects of the changes as you progress on the road to enlightenment. For many of you, once you make a step forward, you feel excited. But then fear grabs you once again, and you make a half step backward. Such is the way when there is spiritual change of this magnitude. Thus I tell you, when you take a half step back, do not be alarmed, and do not let your progress suffer so. Just accept and realize that those half steps backwards can end up pushing you further in the right direction.

Let's look at it this way. If you want to judge your success thus far, ask yourself this. Are you kinder? Are you feeling more loving towards others, to every living thing including the earth itself? Do you love yourself more? Do you desire to smile and laugh more? Do you want to help others, and do you enjoy seeing others happy and well? Do you desire to lift up the spirits of others? Do you feel in love with kindness? If you answer "yes" to these questions, you are choosing love.

When you choose love your energies are focused on love, which through the Law of Attraction creates more love in your life. It creates more love through the people and situations you attract from seemingly chance occurrences, by the increasingly delightful exchanges with family, friends, and strangers, and from the happy surprises you encounter as if sent by magic.

Then boom, something upsetting or downright bad happens, and you wonder what did you do wrong. You think you must have deserved this punishment. This sets you a half step backwards because the fears, doubts, and negative thinking return. "Oh, I'm not as evolved as I thought," you think. Out of habit, you just go right into that negative thinking again and become filled with anger or disgust towards self and/or others. So what do you do?

You see that this occurred because it was the next step; maybe another karmic lesson needs to be learned. And when you realize it, you want to learn it well and be done with it. Is this easy? No, perhaps not, but it is much easier when you realize it was a destined occurrence to propel you further in your growth. You see things from a spiritual perspective, and you can piece it all together; why it happened, how did you react, how could you better react, and so on.

Then, as you work your way through it, you tell yourself that if something like this happens again, you will first watch your reaction. Will it be fear-based? If so, what steps can you take to transmute that energy into love? Then you ask what is the lesson to be learned? How can you master this? What has the pattern been and how can you break it? Is it that you let people step all over you? Do you give to others always before yourself? Are you not giving enough to others? Do you love yourself enough? Do you close yourself off to others? Do you judge others?

You often figure out the lesson by recognizing a

pattern. If you have been in judgment of others all your life, you may keep attracting people in your life who judge you. First it will be subtle, and if you don't notice the connection and understand that you attract this to you so that you can learn from it and drop the behavior, then people will be out and out judging you to the point it may hurt and embarrass you. If you still don't notice, you may find yourself in court with a judge judging you, and then, maybe then, when it has become a more serious situation, you get it. You make the connection.

You forgive yourself, and you forgive all the people who "got in your face" to show you this lesson so that you could stop judging others, which thus created spiritual growth. Then you feel on top of the world because you came so far and you're feeling so good; and then boom, something awful happens again. What did you do? Why did this now happen? You feel you can't catch a break after all your hard work, and now this? More punishment?

No, it is not more punishment. It is the next lesson. It is the next thing to clear from you that no longer serves your growing self. But it may take awhile to understand, and you go into fear, confusion, doubt, and denial moving a half step backward until your spirit taps you on the head saying, "This is just another step." You did well on that, and now you have to work on this. You will hopefully call on the angels for help to recognize what you need to see and heal within yourself. You feel deep relief when you realize that you did nothing wrong, but just clearing out more of the old you.

And so this process goes on, as all of you are experiencing this now. And it's happening so quickly, one lesson on top of another so you can be ready for the shift. No one is spared from this process or you would not be on the earth plane. There are things you need to learn. You are shedding the old, the parts of you that are not conducive to living in the Golden Age. You get to a point where you are in control of your reactions, as you see everything from a higher perspective, almost as if you are playing a game. And when you complete it, you play a different game, and you keep doing so until games are no longer needed, and you can just be. You can live in love and Light and have a peaceful existence. You all deserve this, and you can have this.

Remember, you are not alone. Your angels can give you comfort and such extraordinary signs that they are with you. That alone helps you deal with any difficulty, but on top of that, they can help you when you ask. They very much want to help you and can ease your transition tremendously. Regardless, they love you and celebrate your every accomplishment, as every accomplishment spreads Light around the world. What you do for you, you do for the earth itself.

Clearing and shedding the last parts of the old us is not easy. I don't know how I could do it, personally, without my angels' help now. Looking back, I wish I asked for their help much more often, although it is an unhealthy act to hold regrets of any kind. Life has been very difficult since the two plus years prior to writing this book, and I was exhausted and in survival mode most of the time. My daughter suffered from a chronic health condition, which, most thankfully, she has since recovered from. I was so distraught over her daily challenges that I sometimes had a hard time connecting spiritually; even with Archangel Michael.

In my distress, I sought help from an angelic channeler named Jeannie Barnes. My sessions with Jeannie seemed to be my only refuge at the time. I felt such solace during those sessions, and through my connection with

Jeannie, I received many loving messages from the angels. Those moments with the angels, and the communications received from them, filled me with love and gave me the hope and strength I needed to continue to mentally and emotionally help my daughter overcome her challenges.

My daughter achieved tremendous spiritual growth, and together we constantly sought the reasons why she endured this challenge and learned to bless them all. She knew from the time she was quite young that she wanted to be a healer. Conventional medicine could not help her, and, not so surprisingly, this put her in connection with all kinds of alternative healers so that she could learn the art of healing. This helped to nurture and develop her inherent abilities, and in many ways she learned to heal herself with the help of these healers. She also learned to form such beautiful relationships with her angels.

We traversed many mountains and valleys together. It seemed that every time the difficulties seemed to fade somewhat, just like that we'd be "hit" again with another set of challenges to address. While I took several half steps backward, as Michael calls them, my daughter was much more accepting. It was a period of tremendous growth for my family. Without our angels, and the Universe providing amazing signs that would guide us through her journey by putting the right healers and appropriate guidance before us, it would have been many times more difficult.

The grand lessons that we learned together were to never go it alone, to always ask for help, and to be in a state of constant gratitude for the help we receive. Toward the latter part of this challenge, I was able to reconnect with Archangel Michael. I will never again lose touch with this most important connection no matter what I am faced with. I know much better now. We ultimately understood that we would not have learned all these rich spiritual lessons, nor would my daughter be so well prepared to be the beautiful healer she already is, had we not experienced every aspect of this.

*   *   *   *

Imagine an egg, and the egg has a really tough shell. And people go and swipe at it, throw it, hammer at it, trying to break through; yet the egg remains intact. It remains a hard shell, and although your common sense would have you believe you could crack the egg, it remains intact. You are all like that egg. You have a shell around you that some people try to crack, but it is not possible. The shell is your spirit, you soul, and your soul lives on into eternity. No human can break through your soul. They can hammer it and throw it around, but they can't kill it.

Your spirit, your soul, is by far the strongest part of you as it is who you really are. Although you are enduring often intense difficulties during these chaotic times, your soul remains intact. It will get you through anything. So start to seek a closer relationship with who you really are, and draw from this strength. Talk to you. Call on you. Dance with you. Celebrate with you. This starts perhaps with just your imagination. And then one day, you will meet you, and it will be the most real experience of your life. You will meet and know you.

This may be a difficult concept to grasp so let me put this in a way you may better understand. Jesus was a human on earth. He had all the physical functions and needs that you do. He also was self-realized. As the Son of God, He lived as a human who could also perform miracles and do many things that humans could not do. He knew who He really was, and although He had a physical body,

His relationship to His soul was paramount. And this is the way it will be with you, when you become who you really are.

I recently spent a good part of a day researching some wise movers and shakers who are uncovering what is going on behind the scenes in this world and where we are heading. I was led to read articles about an obviously intelligent person who is aware of the dark side of these activities. Although this person was uncovering shocking secrets that have been kept from society, he didn't seem to understand how this plays into the fall, and, thus, the new beginning for all of those who choose it. Rather, he has a very grave idea about what our future holds.

Later this day, I saw the movie *Avatar*. In the movie, Eywa is the deity of the Na'vi people of Pandora, a habitable moon. When the main female character says, "Eywa heard you," and then all the wild animals fought the enemy to help the Na'vi protect their land, I felt intense vibrations moving throughout my body, and I really got it. This mimicked the signs I shared in my previous book, *I Can See Clearly Now,* that we will indeed be saved by the grace of God. Earlier in the movie, this character said that Eywa doesn't take sides and is only concerned with balance. But in the end, their God saved the people and their land. This movie serves as a metaphor of what is to come, in my viewpoint. The only thing that can interfere with free will is God's grace.

I thought of this person who has a wealth of understanding of what is truly occurring behind the scenes third dimensionally, through his mind. It appears he hasn't made the heart connection, though, the spiritual connection, knowing that we will indeed be saved. That the state of the earth is not futile, as he presently believes. We will not destroy ourselves no matter how bad or how impossible these situations are, that we have witnessed or continue to witness. Nothing is stronger than the force of God.

This is the same message I received through a string of profound synchronicities, which I detailed in *I Can See Clearly Now*. I kept receiving signs about Molly Brown, the woman who was "saved" in the sinking of the Titanic as portrayed in the movie, *The Unsinkable Molly Brown*. (Interestingly, and as a side note, the director of the movie *Avatar* also directed *Titanic*.) They were coupled with synchronicities involving the "rose," symbolizing the intensifying energies of the Divine Feminine that are dissolving the aspects of life on earth that no longer serve us.

Although we have been sinking as if we are all, metaphorically, passengers on the Titanic, we will be saved by surrendering to God's grace. We are unsinkable. And we will be imbued with the energies of the "rose," the Divine Feminine, as we enter the Golden Age.

*   *   *   *

There will come a time when you can hear all of us in the Heavenly realms. Yes, you will be able to hear us with your ears. We will have communication between us and it will be glorious. No longer will a veil divide us, and you will marvel at the gift of communication with, literally, all of us. So that is another gift you have to look forward to.

Ever wonder what all of us do here? We serve you. We serve the greater good. We serve God who is in all of you. Does that sound like boring work to just serve others and not the ego self? I tell you that it is by serving others that we serve ourselves. You have not been taught that, for the most part, but that is changing. You are opening your hearts up to others, and when you do so, the natural pro-

gression moves to the desire of serving others.

Life will be so grand when you let go of the need to serve your ego, and rather learn to just be. Your life will be so grand when you acknowledge your shadow side and release all that no longer serves the evolving human. But it will be especially grand when you recreate a world that is filled with Light. Oh, it will be so bright. Yet, it will not take getting used to. You will thrive in the Light. Your bodies will adjust to the Light.

Your spirit will find itself home, and it will be a glorious reunion, with both you and with Heaven. The joy that will be felt would overwhelm you right now, so just take these words as assurances that fill all the parts of you that are tired and hurting. Let the promise of the creation of Heaven on earth be your lifeline to get through your challenges. This will be the greatest story ever told, and you are a part of it.

The greatest story ever told. How lucky are we to be on this planet at this time? It doesn't seem that much about living on earth has been easy; for many of us it has been downright relentlessly difficult. But if we choose love and this new life, we are done with the old ways of being forever! What a relief this is. The last hurrah is challenging, but there is a new dimension at the end of the tunnel that will make all our efforts and hardships extremely worthwhile. I understand that when we move into this new dimension, we will feel cleansed and cleared of the unpleasant memories, and we will be fully rejuvenated to begin a new way of living. The old weights will be lifted so we can begin anew.

*   *   *   *

You are learning to serve others now more than ever. First, you must take care of yourself; you must love and serve yourself so that you are able to help others. As you serve others, be careful what you are doing to feed the ego versus your true self. It is a completely new way to serve others, when ego is out of the way. Serve from the heart without expectation of receiving anything in return. Great things come out of serving without ego.

As a human, you cannot be what a human would consider as perfect, and perfection is not expected! Improvement is expected. Living from the heart is expected. Letting go of the past is expected. Caring about others is expected. These things are expected if you, by free will, are choosing love over fear and creating Heaven on earth, instead of continuing with third dimensional ways of being. However, we don't expect your perfection in these areas, just your pure intention to live in this manner.

It is you who you are accountable for. You are not accountable for a family member or a friend—only you. By the same token, it is not up to you to infringe on others' beliefs or choices. You must respect the free will of others even when they are making different choices. This is not easy. If they ask your opinion or join you in activities that breed a new way of living, that is fine and you are free to share. If they don't ask, you can only just be who you are. If they see your Light and want to find that in themselves and ask you for help, that is great. Just be, just shine your Light, but do not lecture or try to convince when not invited.

And so we see that one of the ways we can improve ourselves and help others at the same time is to live our Light. As Michael points out, living by example is the best way to help others, because free will is something that must be respected. It can be habit to "tell" people what they "should" be doing, and this is very true when it comes to those closest to us, or those who may not see eye to eye with us, and especially true when we see people choosing fear over love. All we need to do is project our love and live our Light. But not allow anyone to dim *your* Light. Some may try, for example, by ridiculing you for your beliefs, and if they do, just agree to disagree. Stay strong in your power.

By this same token, I can personally write this book and I can speak to groups, because people choose to read or hear these messages, but I should not go and stand on a park bench and force my knowledge, beliefs, and way of life on others. I know that people who are genuinely seeking information and guidance to help them through this shift will indeed attract it into their lives, whether it's a teacher, a book, and/or whatever means.

Many of us suffer with perfection issues, myself included with regard to certain aspects of my life, and I was glad that Michael addressed this by explaining that perfection is not expected. And we truly cannot be perfect, no matter how much we wish it so. With this realization comes the understanding that we need to forgive ourselves when we do stray on the path, when we do react with outrage and anger, or when the wrong words come out of our mouths.

*   *   *   *

Mary, my dear treasure. You are embarking on a new ability. And that is the telepathic ability to receive instant information from all of us in the Heavenly realms. You can ask for any one of us beings—angels, Archangels, and any of the Ascended Masters—and you will be able to not just receive, which you have before, but you can also have conversations back and forth. So try this now.

This took me by surprise. I felt I would be able to channel others, but always knew that I would mostly work with Michael. I must now adjust my way of channeling, and rather speak in conversation as he is now describing to me. I will just go with my heart, and not think about this.

"I wish to speak with Jesus."

I am here, my dear child. You are a shining diamond. We see so many of you as these shining diamonds who do not yet know of your brilliance. One day you will though, and we are preparing for your entry into my Father's kingdom.

"What does the biblical saying that there are many mansions in your Father's house mean?"

We love that about you that you always seek to focus on the desirable, as his many mansions are so desirable. In this place that you are creating as we speak, there will be glorious opportunities that you cannot even dream of. What do you think of when you think of a mansion on your earth? That it is a wondrous place to live in? Yes, God will provide you with a wondrous place to live that is beyond your imaginings. You will be rewarded in ways that your mind cannot understand right now, but I do ask you to just feel the possibilities in your heart. Feel the wonder of the new and beautiful existence that God and the Heavens can provide for all of you. Feel what it will be like to live in a most wondrous place. The wonders will be felt from the heart and in connection to your soul. So get used to this way of being. Use your heart to begin to understand what God has in store for you.

"It is a relief to be given permission to live from the heart. I know I speak for many who naturally have desired to live that way, but society does not really permit it, or they look down on it, whether in our work or in family life or anywhere. It has been seen as weak and unwise. In my heart, I am feeling such relief to start living this way now."

No one knows better than each of you how to access the heart. It is an instantaneous connection once you make the choice. When you are heart-centered you attract people in your life who are heart-centered, and this helps you stay connected in this way. Someone who is not centered in this way can come along and possibly cause you to be ego-centered again, yet there will come a time when you will not be challenged in this way. You will get to the desired point of no return where you remain heart-centered. Keep making the choice to be heart-centered and see what happens. See what you attract in your life that will fill you with such gratitude for, which then attracts only more of the same.

"What can you say to people who don't believe I am really communicating with you and, thus, don't believe that they, too, can experience this blessed communication?"

The belief that any one of you cannot have a conversation with God, myself, or any other Master, is just that, a belief. Experience is what can change a belief, but that doesn't necessarily occur either. If they have the experience for themselves, then they still may not believe it really occurred. You cannot convince anyone to believe anything in this book or anything in any book. It is up to each of you to have your minds open to the possibility of truth. It is up to you to request this type of communication. All you have to do is ask.

"I was one of the ones second-guessing everything I heard when I was learning to channel. However, as I read the messages, I was surprised at their beauty and the speaking of things that were not in my mind."

Get used to the beauty. As you all gain the experience, you grow your trust. As you grow your trust, you will delight at where your trust will take you. Again I say, do this from the heart. Your heart holds wisdom, feelings, and the knowingness of what is true.

"Thank you, Jesus."

"Michael, I'm getting that from now on you wish for me to communicate in just this way, as a conversation. I noticed that we've slipped into conversation several times before, without my even realizing it or thinking about it at the time."

It is the natural progression as you began by just receiving my messages. Now, as you are more comfortable, you can see that we can have a constant and fluid two-way conversation that flows just where it should flow.

CHAPTER 5

Conversations with Michael

At this point, I will switch from channeling messages to now having conversations with Michael. Again, communicating with our angels, Archangels, Ascended Masters, and guides is a birthright of all human beings,. If I can do it, so can you if you so desire (and if you haven't yet).

"Michael, this is when I feel so confident that I am hearing you well, when things suddenly shift, and I'm now taking this new direction of having conversations with you. I was thinking that Chapter 4 would be the last chapter of the book, comprised of all your new messages. I'm trying not to have expectations, but couldn't help myself."

Yes, you did have that expectation, but you were immediately open to the new format. And this represents the way many others may experience communication from the Heavenly realms. They will first just receive the words they need to hear. Once they establish trust in the process, the natural progression is a conversation as if talking to a friend. You can talk to us just as if we are friends, because we are your friends. There is nothing you cannot ask us. The only reason we may keep something from you is because you may not be ready. Your mind isn't capable of understanding everything we wish to tell you. That is why this book can only give you a sneak peak, as you would call it. This is what many of you can understand right now, and for some, it is already too much. To them I say your understanding will increase in time. You may feel shock over the changes I have described, but in time you will see that things cannot remain the same and you are all, on some level, creating these changes. You chose this beautiful destiny, and so, as long as you keep an open mind, eventually the truth will reveal itself.

"How can we be more receptive to these types of gifts? It seems that many of us may not even feel worthy of talking to any of you."

That is because you don't know who you really are! If you did, you would be enjoying these gifts now. As you increase in vibrational frequency, the communications become easier. You can start by asking simple "yes" and "no" questions. Start simply if you wish. Do this now. Just ask any being from the Light a simple question you have and then either see, hear, or know the answer of "yes" or "no." With your inquisitive nature, you may get excited when you start getting the yes or no so easily, and start to ask open-ended questions. Just set this book down reader, and see what transpires. Go with your heart.

"I hope this inspires many to communicate with Heaven if they aren't already doing so. For me, there is nothing I'd rather do."

That is because you have figured out that this is the best way to get your questions answered. You grew up having a very deep respect and trust for authority, institutions, et cetera, but you lost that respect and trust after being greatly disillusioned and disappointed time and time again. You turned your questions to God and the angelic realms. Here you have found your comfort, your truth, your deepest love and respect. You went from living as one who lived deep-seated in society's demands and beliefs to being just a visitor of this planet, ready for the major shift and change you eventually knew would one day arrive.

"Yes, it is like that expression, 'I'm in this world and not of it.' I really resonate with that, as so many of us do."

When you realize that all of you chose to come here to help make this shift, it helps you cope with what you call "the insanity." You are here to serve, and while that means being aware of the woes of society, you've always had control over how much that affects you. You can always turn off the television, stop reading the newspaper, walk away from gossip, buy safer and healthier food, or stop working for a corrupt company. These choices help significantly and you can always re-choose again and again.

"Often, they are habits that need to be broken. However, it seems that it is getting easier to release habits."

That is absolutely true. People are rethinking how they spend their day, what their choices are, and what resonates and no longer resonates with them; a constant reassessment that ultimately leads to a change in their actions and behaviors. The reason that it is easier is because as they are already releasing much of their past, those habits which are connected to their old beliefs and actions, just dissolve naturally right along with them.

"Releasing friends and people in your life who you no longer connect with is more difficult."

It is difficult until you look at the bigger picture. You are here on earth to grow and learn. If someone is unsupportive, is knocking down your ideas, work, or dreams, speaks negatively, and such, they are not helping you in your growth. Yes, you are used to them, you may have some laughs with them, yet your time together may be superficial and forced, and that does not serve either of you. Especially during these transformative times, it is vital to consider how you spend your time and whom you spend it with.

"What if that includes family members?"

Your family is your family; however, you have to consider the same thing. You don't have to completely shut anyone out of your life, but you may choose to change the amount of time you spend with them, and that includes your thoughts about them. If a family member is knocking you down, affecting your self-esteem, judging you relentlessly, et cetera, you need to watch your self-thoughts and not allow another to change how you feel about yourself. As you get closer to understanding who you really are, those negative self-thoughts dissolve readily.

"It has been said that the greatest negative self-thought, or the common denominator of all negative self-thoughts, is that one is 'unlovable.' Thus, it seems impossible for this misbelief to exist once we connect with our souls."

When you connect with the Heavenly realms, our first and foremost message to you is that we love you. The love would feel so overwhelming to you if you could allow yourselves to feel it. For someone to think they are unlovable is a great misunderstanding. One day they will understand, when as you say, they connect with who they really are. Until then, as they learn to be love, they learn to love themselves.

*   *   *   *

"Michael, you put that very clear image of a fire alarm in my third eye as I was trying to wake myself up!"

Yes, and it worked.

"Yes, it did! I found it so funny that I woke immediately. I thought the doorbell sound you ring in my mind to wake me was funny, but you really surprised me here. You know I love a good laugh. I was having a hard time waking up as it was, yet I *heard* your humorous warning that 'if you don't wake up, I'm going to pull this alarm!' Actually, I prefer the doorbell technique. Your surprise this morning made me further realize I really have no idea just what you angels can do, just what you are capable of creating for us."

That was the idea. It was our creative way to show you that. We can use sounds and images in many different ways to get your attention. You know that we can whisper things to you.

"Yes, for years I've known this, but I am not always sure whether the whispers are coming from the Heavens, if it's my Higher Self, or just my conscious, thinking self. When the thought, which may have been a whisper, leads me to some synchronicity, then I'm sure it is not me. For instance, you may whisper to get in the car now, and as soon as I do, I'm at the perfect place and at the perfect time for the synchronicity to occur."

"For instance, one morning I had a knowingness to get

in the car. I didn't know why, but I trusted my gut. I felt led to drive a mile from my house toward my bank. At a stoplight, and just a few blocks from my bank, I suddenly saw right in front of me a bunch of small, rectangular pastel-colored papers flying in the air. Just as I questioned to myself whether it was 'Monopoly' money because that's exactly what it looked like, I turned my head to the left, and the wind caused by cars driving by blew over a game board cover with the word 'Monopoly'! The money was flying everywhere as cars drove over it. It was a strange and, yet, incredible sight."

"Once the traffic light turned green, and I drove this same path, I saw in my rear view mirror that the money was kicked up into the air in the trail behind me. It was quite a scene to witness. Whenever I imagine financial abundance, I see money falling on me from above so this was a stunning visual in my present reality. I was concerned about finances at that time, and I felt you were showing me that all would be well by guiding me to that perfect place and time for the synchronicity to occur."

Yes, that's just one of the many reasons why we may whisper things to you.

"You also whisper songs to me, especially when I'm waking up. I wake with a line of a song on my lips, and it always has a message for me."

We whisper many things to you. With permission from you, we can interfere in a good way and help you create what you wish. We whisper to go here, call that place, go to this website—all to find the people and connections you need.

"Just as you did yesterday. I was sure you guided me to read the interviews of that whistleblower who is very successfully revealing the dark side of some corporations and politics, but doesn't champion hope for this world. I read this just prior to watching the movie Avatar, which to me was another sign that God will indeed save us; signs that I continue to notice in so many ways. You continually help direct me to these conclusions."

This is true. There is much more we will point out, even if repetitious, so that you will all really understand our message and call to you. So that you understand that you are about to transition into a whole new life. We are here to help you through this process. When you listen to the signs of the Universe, you will be shown the way to the truth.

"That is why synchronicity is so important. Synchronicity cannot lie. It is a magical revealing of the true state of things or a true reading of energies."

Synchronicity is a gift to the seeker. When in touch with synchronicity, one can really explore the state of things in one's life and the outside world. Sometimes, the synchronicity is meant for the individual. For instance, if someone thinks of someone, and then a moment later sees them at the grocery store. Other times, a synchronicity can reflect an event or even a calamity that is going on in the world. You experienced many synchronicities prior to 9/11 that made you realize something awful was about to occur, even though you had no idea of the magnitude the disaster would be.

"I'll never forget that. Synchronicity has always given me a 'heads up' on things. It prepares me."

Not everyone feels that way. They may not want to know so they may not allow themselves to decipher the sign, and try to ignore the fact they are being forewarned.

"I'd much rather know so that I can be prepared. It lessens the shock, and I can start asking my angels for help. Also, I get previews when something to celebrate is on the horizon. Of course, I welcome those, especially so."

And we celebrate with you. Do you know what else synchronicity can provide and this is something you have never touched on.

"No, what?"

The noticing of them actually raises your vibration. When you acknowledge them, you are raising your vibrational frequency because you are tuning into higher states of being. Thus, this is another benefit of being what you call a "synchronist."

"I never thought of it in that way."

As I described in *I Can See Clearly Now*, and wish to stress the importance of here, is that when we hold negative thoughts or fears about something, we can actually attract synchronicity perfectly reflecting the negativity. It is truly amazing how this works.

*   *   *   *

You are worn, Mary. You are worn from the confusing energies all around. Imagine me giving you an orange. You bite through it and the outside is bitter, way too difficult to swallow, but the inside is so sweet. You have tasted some of the bitter, but are about to taste the sweet. Just keep on going, as you are right there. Please don't hesitate. We will together get you through this; yet I tell you that you are right there. You'll see what I mean. Just hold on. And look for a miracle today, just for you.

A miracle did end up occurring today, several hours after Michael's suggestion to look for one. After picking my daughter up from school, we were on the way home, and I was shocked at the sight of a perfectly shaped cloud in the sky, as it looked just like a jet plane. If that weren't enough, right below the cloud was the same image, but the cloud wasn't quite as dense, yet it was almost exactly the same shape. The clouds both looked just like a jet with a very well defined tail. As we both watched with amazement, the clouds quickly dissipated in just seconds and there were hardly any remnants left of the clouds! I knew that was the miracle that Michael spoke of, and it gave me such joy.

While witnessing the "jet clouds," I recalled my angels recently telling me that I would soon be rewarded with a little vacation for my efforts with this book. I wondered if this were Michael's way of also showing me that I would be getting a little break away. If so, it would indeed be unexpected, because I have no plans to travel for several months.

Note: A few days later, I found myself booking a totally unexpected trip!

"Can synchronicity unveil what the new age will be like?"

Of course, as it has, yet it may take a very advanced seeker with an open mind to notice. Synchronicity is always there whether someone is noticing or not, as synchronicity is an unstoppable energetic creation and force. It is what it is, and that is why truth seekers should look to synchronicity for their answers.

"Can you give any advice to us truth seekers who want the validation?"

Let us help guide you to your notice and understanding of them. Synchronicities can be easily missed. They can most certainly be misunderstood. Call on us to help you. We use synchronicity ourselves to give you messages. One day, it will be as easy as a conversation like this for us to communicate with you. Yet, signs are a glorious gift and can give you much comfort and direction. Keep blessing each sign as they come and honor them for the sacred gifts they are.

"What happens when we don't show gratitude for synchronicity, signs from our angels, or for any of the sacred gifts bestowed on us?"

You become stagnant because you take things for granted; whereas gratitude increases the flow of gifts. When you are in that blessed state, it affects the energy of flow to you in a most beneficial way. Do you remember when you were so excited about moving to New Mexico? You were in such a state of gratitude that you attracted this flow of so many good things that surrounded your move.

"That is so true. It was such a gloriously happy time. Even though we moved across the country, it was such an easy and joyful move. I remember there was this flow of abundance, and we were gifted with so many things on top of already being beyond content. It was as if the Universe was conspiring to make me and my family happy! My feeling now is that was a taste of what it will be like when we all shift. We'll all be living in this love energy, which gratitude is such a large part of, and which will create feelings of bliss for all."

So be it.

*   *   *   *

"When reading different channelings and interpretations regarding the shift, 2012, etc., I am surprised at all the conflicting information. Why is everyone's interpretations differing from each other's, including ours."

I've been waiting for you to ask that question. While most channels' intentions are true, and they strive for clear information, the messages coming through sometimes get distorted because of the channel's beliefs and, perhaps, their own fears, but also because the information may seem so different or impossible to believe. So they skew the information to fit what would be acceptable, without really meaning to. Further, some of the information is potential, and will not necessarily manifest. You are chosen because you strive so hard for truth. When things don't make sense to you, you question and constantly request clarity. None of your minds are capable of understanding everything as it will be, and that's why I stated earlier to readers that what we discuss is only part of, a taste of, the new reality. Our combined mission is to help others prepare for the changes, to guide them toward the help they will need; but none of you are really going to have a firm understanding of all that there is to know yet.

Also, there is no way to fully state exactly how things will be because you are still, all together, in creation mode. All the details of how things will be are not yet set in stone, especially when it comes to timing. So do not ask this channel, readers, about timing because she is not going to be able to tell you. You, Mary, get frustrated because you want all the answers, but I tell you that you will get them when it is appropriate. The fact that you need to be love, shed the old parts of you that no longer serve you, practice gratitude, forgive those you have yet to forgive; these requirements are set and so many of you are beautifully moving in this direction.

"I do want all the answers, but will remain patient now while keeping my heart open to the information that will come through at the appropriate time."

I say this to all of you—when you do feel frustrated, put the books or the computer down, and go within and there you will find your answers. This book is a guide, an impetus to help you connect you with you. But going within is your key to the knowledge and understanding you seek. Do the internal work, and you will reap many rewards.

"Well, I think the word 'work' scares people. We are feeling overwhelmed as it is."

It is by going within that you make sense of all that is overwhelming you. You find ways to pare and trim things from your life that no longer serve you. These are overwhelming times, but what can also help is to make a constant effort to simplify your life. Many of you are feeling the push to move into a smaller home, to rid of clutter, and to make things as easy and simple as possible. I hold no judgment of one way or the other, but I do maintain that it behooves you to embrace simplicity wherever you can.

"Society breeds us to complicate our lives it seems, to constantly purchase things and keep up with the latest and greatest, and we are overwhelmed with information and advertising."

As you grow on your path, you lessen the focus on the material and stop listening to society who tries to tell you what you should and should not do, and rather listen to the wealth of information that comes from within.

Can you get into the habit of meditating when you have those feelings of overwhelm? Just go do this now yourself, Mary, for you are feeling very overwhelmed.

"Yes, even going to the grocery store was overwhelming. I feel that my awareness is heightened and I am extra sensitive to my surroundings. It's as if everything in the third dimension is too much. So I will meditate now."

(I meditated for about thirty minutes.)

"I truly do feel calmer now, but much more than that. When I called forth the bliss and ecstasy, I felt it running through my body, incredibly so. It came in waves. I meditated on my third eye, and, just out of the blue, the sensations would overtake me. Then it would subside, and then happen again. Why does it happen like that?"

Because that is what you can comfortably handle at

this point. As you continue to practice this, you will feel the effects more continual perhaps, depending on how your body reacts on any given day.

"Does this actually help me raise my vibration?"

Anything that brings love and Light to your being raises your vibration, so the answer to your question is, most definitely, yes. Anytime you meditate, no matter what the motivation, whether you wish to receive answers or receive the bliss, you are raising your vibration because you are moving a step upward from the third dimension.

Think of it in these terms: whenever you think, say, do, or feel anything that is of love and Light, you will raise your vibration. Your kindness to a stranger, your gratitude for the sunset, your giving of your time and energy to help another, your sending a prayer out, your caring of the planet, your heart-felt smiles, hugs, and kisses; all that comes from love and Light will benefit you in unseen ways. Or at least they may seem unseen right now.

"I am so in love with kindness. When I witness displays of loving kindness, just as when I demonstrate it myself, it fills me with such joy. I have to say, I am seeing more kindness in my life right now than I ever have before."

You are seeing love and Light manifest. You are seeing the changes and transformations actually appearing before your very eyes, and it is only going to become stronger and more apparent as more choose love. You will mirror each other and learn from each other the new ways of being. It is a contagious thing, a wonderfully contagious happening that we are observing with much joy. And the beautiful thing is that the feelings are real. They are not fake. The love is real and people like being real. They are slowly getting to know who they real-ly are.

"As I recognize more loving kindness out there, I'm

also noticing that the non-loving situations with people spewing anger, rudeness, and thoughtlessness are no longer affecting me like they used to. Either I'm not seeing people in these states as often because I'm not attracting it around me, or even when I do, I just naturally distance myself from it. It's not one hundred percent this way, yet there is a definitely a shift here."

And this will only increase as you grow your state of love, along with others doing the same. You will no longer be affected by negative energies like you were. It is as if you are all on the same earth, but there is a magnet that brings like-minded, love filled people together. And anything that does not flow with your vibration just slides off of you; it no longer sticks. You do not get easily triggered. You just accept and stay focused on love and Light.

"This seems to be the easy part of our ascension, our knowing of who we really are. When it's so natural and contagious, there is such an easy flow to this."

You'll find that as you raise your vibration, which means you have also cleared out that which no longer serves the new you, everything will get much easier. Life will mirror the state of your vibration. Always think in terms of mirrors. Like attracts like. It is a simple concept to understand. Simply be the mirror of that you wish to see around you.

"That's a beautiful way to think of it. I will remember that."

There is another way to share the loving kindness you speak of with others. Whenever someone you know of— whether a friend, family member, or a stranger you meet— is suffering in any way, hold him or her in your thoughts for but a moment, and whisper "I love you" to them from your heart. That may sound silly, yet the truth is that on some level they will hear it, they will feel it, and it will help comfort them.

Whisper "I love you" to the earth itself, or to an area on earth that is suffering. When you perform this act, you raise your own vibration, as well as the vibration of that which is receiving. Love breeds love, Light breeds Light; enjoy these most contagious energies to behold.

"I also whisper, 'I love you' to my angels, and all the angels who are helping us. There is this feeling of frustration I have for them, as they desire to help us, but so relatively few are requesting their help. That included me until recent years. It's hard to convince others that they truly can help us since there is no tangible proof that they exist. We are visual people, for the most part, and we almost need to see them with our own eyes in order to believe."

And one day you will! Until then, they must have a willingness to give the angels a chance to prove to them they really can serve them. And then, as you say, "the proof is in the pudding."

"This is why I've learned to favor my own experience over scientific proof of the mystical. Science isn't proving to us the existence of angels, and so we can only learn by experience. We do not have to look outside of ourselves for answers or validation. I've learned to trust what I receive from within and what I witness through universal messages of synchronicity. When the 'proof in the pudding' shows that our angels are helping us again and again, we can each draw our own conclusions."

"The best way I've learned to begin this process is to ask our angels for signs. They are whispering for us to look at the clock 'right now' and we witness an interesting sequence of numbers, like the angels' numbers '444,' or other repetitive sets of numbers. When this happens again and again, we know we are surrounded in love, surrounded by the angels. Lately, it seems that their ways of reaching us and helping us are all even more glorious and powerful than ever before."

As the veil thins, you will receive more from your angels. They can help you in more significant ways, help you to see more of yourself, and can provide you with more magic and miracles than ever before. This is a steady increase that is continually unfolding, and as this happens, you will be manifesting more easily and in a grander way.

"What is not to like about this news? I hope this inspires readers to truly work with them. I consider those of us who work with our angels as pioneers finding creative ways to grow our relationships with our angels. It feels like a creative process to me."

That is your soul at work. You soul is communicating to you, asking of you to be more creative on your spiritual path. Your soul will guide you on your path with the angels until one day you will be talking to them face to face!

"Now that is really opening up my mind. We really need to be at the ready to release attachments to our beliefs, because as we become more and more aware, our understanding of everything is going to change. I realize that my present beliefs are based only on what I know, and that's why I'm continually reassessing them, allowing myself to think again."

You say "think," but you mean "feel." You are very feeling, and go by your heart much more often than you realize. Yes, this is true and an important concept to be aware of, that your beliefs will have to evolve with you.

"It does not sound as if we'll have to work so hard to seek understanding. We will just know things. True?"

Your soul knows, and thus, when you connect with

116

your soul, you connect with its wisdom. You will be increasingly connected to the angelic realms, as well. So yes, you will find that your understanding of the world around you will come much easier, and also because truth comes easily from a love and Light filled earth. You who are on earth are presently being bombarded with dishonesty and untruths coming from so many directions that you often do not know what to believe about earthly things, let alone spiritual ones...this will change.

"As we become more connected to the Heavenly realms, will we be able to communicate with loved ones who have passed?"

The word "death" will seem inappropriate when you experience for yourself where your loved ones have gone. Yes, you will be able to communicate to them, and they will be such grand reunions.

"So many people seem to be, well, let's call it 'transitioning' to the other side. Why is this so?"

There are many reasons, many you would have no idea of from your perspective; but I can tell you there are some who chose to be on our side of the veil prior to the shift occurring.

"We need so much help, and we have so much help. I just hope people use this help."

And that is why the Lightworkers are working so hard to shine the Light on all there is, and support everyone through this. You can only shine Light and guide those people who choose to listen. When they see such Light coming from the Lightworkers, they may want it too. Many are attracted to it, and others are repelled by the Light, as well. Some Lightworkers have moments where they feel invisible when they are in public, as some ignore the Light and don't want to see it. All one can do is just be, keep shining, not forcing in any manner, but just simply be.

"I have experienced that invisible feeling when out in public. Although, I was sure it was because some people treat me differently because I am overweight and it repels them."

Your beliefs about that could have helped create those situations to occur, but your Light has indeed kept some people you encounter from seeing you. The Light has a way of making people face things they don't want to face. They are more comfortable in the dark. The Light simply makes them feel uncomfortable. So that is their free choice, and you need to not let it affect you in any way.

"Well, I have learned to not care as much, to not worry about what people may think of me. I have wasted so much energy in this way. In these times of great change, I finally realized that I need to stop worrying about peoples' reactions to my work, most especially. You have helped me to do so."

And that is a two-way street when it comes to learning. They may learn to not judge while you may learn to release attachment to peoples' reactions. Often, people just see how a given situation is affecting them, but there is also a lesson involving the other person or persons involved. Given that people desire acceptance and understanding, this is a difficult lesson to learn. But always send love to that person who judged you and let them move on, as they will get another opportunity to learn not to judge. Throwing anger out to them does not serve you or them. Just see it from a higher perspective, that they are learning non-judgment.

"This just reverberates throughout my whole being. The idea of viewing it as both of our learning paths and, thus, not taking things personally! Life keeps showing me to stop taking things personally, and that is hard for us sensitive types. It is also a huge relief. We are all in constant learning mode, but I'm feeling that we will no longer need all the drama that comes with learning as we transition into the new energy."

For those who choose to adapt to the new energy, they most definitely won't attract such drama anymore. Life will still hold challenges and growth potential, but as you evolve and become who you really are, the impetuses that normally create drama won't be triggered. You will enjoy peace between countries and peace between each other.

"It seems that peace will be too boring for some, as I believe that some people really like the drama on some level. It keeps them from being bored."

People will no longer be identifying with their egos, but with their hearts. And their hearts will collectively steer them toward the manifestations of peace; they will demand it and it shall be.

The earth is not used to this, no being is used to this, and the move toward peace will send shock waves of love all over the planet. Every thing will be filled with high levels of love and Light that will create a point of no return.

Do you know what this creates? It creates the opportunity to fully experience love in such a deep way, you would not dare desire to return to the old ways. You will be in such great celebration over your accomplishment, and you will find it difficult to stay grounded in the earth. This will be your challenge, as you will feel "swept off your feet" in love with the new earth.

You will have to recalibrate your energies to remain grounded, and we will help you. You will feel a greater sense of community than ever before, and that includes your connection with the higher realms. You will feel supported and loved, and so utterly joyous that fear no longer remains in your hearts.

"Although I believe what you are saying, it is not easy to imagine with all the crazy insanity of what is going on."

The world is being brought down to its knees, for that is the only way this change can occur. The insanity needs to be seen, truly uncovered, so that everyone knows the truth of the atrocities that have been forced on human life and the earth itself. As these secrets are uncovered, I implore you to celebrate their uncovering rather than focus on the atrocities themselves because you want to stay out of fear and negativity.

You cannot change what happened. You can only understand, see the true picture, and then celebrate the demise of these behaviors and their inability to ever occur on Mother earth again. Stay in the positive flow and do not get caught up in all the anger and disgust. Many of you have already been aware of many of these atrocities, or the possibility that they did indeed exist. So some will be less surprised than others. Either way, you have a choice in your reaction.

"It has taken my whole life up until now to really get it, to watch my reactions. They are very telling of my state of mind and my belief system when I'm honest about my reactions to things."

I have something to share with you, and your reaction to this will be most positive. Think of what it would be like living as an animal in the wild. You have to fight for your sustenance. Your shelter may be bulldozed and destroyed. You are born into having natural enemies. You have difficulties that throw you into fear and attachment, not knowing where your next meal will come from and if something was out to get you. The survival rate is best for the "fittest," and the "lesser" are at a great disadvantage and at greatest risk. There is camouflage, hiding, and constant efforts to not be seen by prey. Life in the wild has generally mirrored humanity. Watch how life in the wild will also evolve to mirror the new ways of the human.

"Oh, I never made the connection that the wild is mirroring humankind. It makes so much sense now. I always had a hard time witnessing and understanding the circle of life, accepting that wild animals had to kill down the food chain to survive. Just like so many of us have such difficulty understanding war. I cannot imagine how wildlife will evolve to mirror the new and improved human, but I find this preview absolutely fascinating."

There is so much that will change and it is appropriate that all not be shared at one time. You don't need all the details right now; just know that the road you are heading on will not disappoint in any way. This is the gift to humanity that was promised, and you are starting to get glimpses of the new. Celebrate each and every one, and be joyful. Things will happen quickly and you will honor those of us in Heaven by accepting our pride in all you have accomplished.

~~~~~~

At this time, Metatron has a message:
Dear beings of Light. For that is what you are becoming, and in the Now you already are. You shine with such brilliance that in unseen ways your whole world is lit up. Just wait until everyone who has chosen this path has firmly stepped into their new roles as evolving humans.

Do you know what our biggest wish for you is? That you, as soon as you can allow yourselves, give up the belief that you are just a mere human. That belief has kept you far from attaining the brilliant knowledge of who you really are. As you evolve into beautiful Light beings, you will behold God's essence in much greater ways than you have, so called mere human. You will shine with new

121

abilities and capabilities that will be bestowed on you, and you will feel such greater connection with God.

This is what we want you to understand: how worthy you all are of knowing and truly experiencing this connection to God, the Source of all that is, as we too experience in the angelic kingdom. There is love and Light and peace because we know we are a part of Source, and there is no separation. I, Metatron, assure all who choose this path will know and experience this true connection that has always been yours. It will light up your hearts with such intensity. You will know what true bliss is. I Am Metatron.

Note: Just before Metatron's message came through, there was a very loud sound just outside my front door and I was sitting only five feet away. There was no one there, nor anything I could see that would have caused this. I then realized this sound represented that a very huge presence was "at my door," and I am grateful for his message. He continued:

Yes, Mary, as you know by now, we use sounds and images to get your attention. Does this give you an idea of how we can influence matter and earthly things to not only alert you, but to help you in a multitude of ways? Even you, who are a grand messenger for the angels, do not know all of what we are capable of.

"I want to know, and yet I feel that list keeps growing as we grow. Let me say that I wholeheartedly choose to understand and experience all the wonderful signs and gifts that angels can bestow on us."

One by one, all of those who also intend this awareness, and other messengers like yourself, will continue to experience the ways we can show ourselves, and what we can do. And you will then share with others.

"Nothing thrills me more than to experience this, and I am filled with gratitude for your gifts."

You thrill the angels with your delight, and the delight of those who welcome the same.

"Life changes when we let our angels in. I know that in my personal life. They bring peace and calm and love into all our life situations."

If you knew the amount of love they have for you, it would overwhelm you. Their love is unconditional, and that is the only kind of love they know.

Quan Yin wishes to speak:

Yes, it is I, Quan Yin. I come in so gently that Mary is wondering if this is really me, and I tell her it is so. I'm known to be the goddess of compassion, but I tell you I am here for you in all ways. You can call on me and I will support you and help you through all the profound adjustments you're making. I love each and every one of you, and I know your hearts. Whatever tears at or breaks your heart, I can come in to help heal it. Love heals all, and all of us angels have so much love for you and want to give you comfort and healing. Call on us anytime, and we will be there the moment of your request. Move toward love in everything you do, everything you speak, and how you treat each other. Let love be your guiding force. When you do so, you will feel a grand difference take shape in your lives.

"Thank you, Quan Yin, for your beautiful and gentle message."

"Michael, when I call on the angels sometimes they step in and totally fix a situation, and other times I feel we are working together. How do I know when I am to be a part of fixing a problem or situation?"

You are always working with the angels, as it should be viewed as a combined, mutual effort. When it's for your highest good, as it must always be for your highest good, we can sometimes grace you with a miracle, and it seems

123

effortless on your part. However, always think of it in terms of working as a unit, and not just having everything done for you; as almost always you must be active in the change or whatever it is you need our help with on your path.

"Why is it so hard to remember to ask? I know that I still sometimes forget, and feel I have to handle things on my own."

Because this is the way it has been, not just in this life, but all your lifetimes. You have adopted a new way of seeing and living now, and this includes consciously choosing to work with your angels. One day, it will become second nature, and you will not even have to think about it. You will call on us immediately when help is needed, feeling as if you are picking up the phone to call your best friend. Except with a mere thought of any of us, we are there.

"As mentioned earlier, and I feel it bears repeating, there are times you cannot interfere."

Yes, and that is a most important point. We cannot interfere by taking away a lesson that needs to be learned or karma that needs to be balanced. However, we can help you through the lessons, the karma, and guide you to the other side of it. We can comfort you through it and make sure you have the support you desire.

Let's say that your lesson is about learning to let go of attachment, and then suddenly you have a break down of your material attachments, one on top of another. Your dream car gets damaged in the parking lot, then you lose your favorite necklace, and you come home to find your television doesn't work. We cannot interfere with the lesson itself and take it away for you, but we can help you understand it and guide you to learning it quickly so you don't have to continue experiencing it again and again.

Remember, when presented with a lesson, and if you don't learn it, you will be presented with it again and again in increasingly challenging ways until you get it. So call on your angels to help you achieve your learning sooner rather than later. Angels can help you grow spiritually in a quicker and more painless fashion when you call on them.

"Ease and effortlessness is what I choose. Is that not what we all desire as we go through such challenges right now? One of my biggest issues has been that I have been a worrier since I was a child. It has been a lifelong task to confront this negative habit. My biggest breakthrough in addressing this has been to ask the angels to help me through this."

Worry has been your main waste of energy throughout your life. It has tired you out; completely exhausted you at times. Most people don't know the main cause of why they worry, yet I tell you that your predisposition to worry—yes, it is a predisposition in your personality and mindset—has mostly to do with some tragic occurrences in your past lives. Even though you are aware of past tragedies and have neutralized the memories, it has become habit, a habit you know you must break.

"You and the angels are helping me with this. As I mentioned, you have taught me recently to not worry about what others think, of my work, especially. When I look at it from a higher perspective, I realized that those who judge are my teachers in making me see that I only need to be concerned about putting out the work, and remain neutral to what others think of my work. These lessons have helped me, but I'm not completely 'cured' of it yet."

You are moving in the right direction, and that is what is important. You know how lessons materialize and how karma can show itself, and that is most necessary for one's growth. Some people who are very heart-centered can sometimes tend to worry because it almost prepares them for any possible occurrences that could surface. Yet, those possibilities often don't occur, and, thus, you have this waste of precious energy.

"And we cannot afford to waste energy, especially now. This leads me to ask, what are some ways we can increase our energy?"

Be in a state of love, as constant a state of love as possible. When you go into fear or any negative state, this zaps you of your energy to such a high degree that it would surprise you if you could see what we can see from our perspective. It robs you of your Light, and your Light is your life force. So another way to put this is to think, say, do, and feel things that you imagine grow your Light. When you grow your Light, you have more energy.

When you smile at someone, when you help another, when you give without condition, when you meditate or pray, when you send love and Light to others, when you are kind to nature, when you are truthful and fair: all these things represent ways that increase Light and, thus, increase your energy.

There are those who say they do these things, and yet still have little energy. Some of you are receiving and transmuting the negative energy of others, and it is to you I say, always take care of yourself first. You are helping to increase the Light by transmuting the negative, but you must protect your beautiful energy, and the angels can help you with this.

"Is this a planned goal of the Lightworkers who transmute energies?"

Yes, they come in with that as their purpose, but they have to learn how to work with it properly so they don't

126

drain themselves of their energy. All over the world, there are so many different roles Lightworkers have found themselves in. Some of you are working with energy, some of you are in mainstream jobs holding the Light, some of you create pockets of Light in the form of humanitarian projects, some of you are writing books and holding seminars, and on and on. You Lightworkers each have your own role. There will be those who join this mission now and into the future, as they awaken to their mission, which may, in some cases, occur as a result of reading this book or other books that awaken them. The numbers of you are multiplying, all contributing in your own ways.

"I honor people in mainstream jobs who have a spiritual understanding and way of life, but go to work every day in an environment that may not welcome this or be conducive to this way of being."

They are honored by us in the angelic realms for their roles, as well. Many feel they should be doing something else, something that is more fulfilling and significant in these changing times. And I tell you that their work of holding the Light in the workplace is vital. They only need to just be an example of the Light, for that is their highest goal, and this quiet state of being can be the most powerful impetus for some to choose this way of being. If they are meant to leave their present roles, and join the forces of Light in other ways, their higher selves will show them the way.

"They seem to find a balance between their roles in the workplace, but also doing what feeds their souls in their own time."

And that is most necessary.

"How about children? How do our children fit into all of this?"

Many of your children are the peacekeepers. They will

direct their Light, naturally, where it needs to be. They will adjust and adapt better than most everyone else, as they are generally not set as far apart from their souls as adults are. They will ease into knowing their souls and living from the soul, and will be examples for all of you. You will look to children as your teachers in many ways and will follow their lead. In a child's heart, you find so much hope and zest for life. They will inspire you to seek that in your own hearts.

"I fully agree that our children are such wonderful teachers. As we continue in our transition, does this mean that children will be more respected and honored than they have been in the past? It has frustrated me, deeply, how some people treat children, especially teenagers, as if they are not worthy of an adult's honor and respect. They don't see their souls and understand that we are all the same, and we are equal. It creates a lack of harmony between the generations."

When you all reunite with your souls, the discord between adults and children will no longer be. There will be such harmony between the generations, and love will abound for all. It is the plight of today's children that is hardest for us to witness, but more and more of you are standing up for children, and your efforts are not unnoticed. Working for the children is sacred work.

"Society doesn't normally speak of age prejudice, but I do think that is what it is. What about other prejudices, of race, sexual orientation, etc.?"

They plain will not exist in the new energy. You're already seeing the shift. Sometimes, there are big upsets, or what may seem as setbacks, in this progression toward acceptance of all. You think things are getting worse, but, in fact, they are improving. Sometimes people, situations, or organizations have to be brought to their knees, which garners awareness, and then things can resettle and change for the better. Awareness and acceptance are the way now. Fear breeds prejudice, so as you release fear, you cannot hold prejudice in your heart. As you connect with your souls, there is no rhyme or reason to prejudice of any kind!

"That is the best news. We will know we have evolved when we all accept each other, each and every one of us, as the beautiful beings we are."

Yes, and the way it used to be will feel like an ancient memory. A memory seen as the stepping stone to understanding whom you really are. You all experienced who you were not, just mere physical beings disconnected from Source and going into fear and prejudice and anything that kept you disconnected, until one day you woke up and saw the Light. And then everything changed forever.

"This time cannot come soon enough."

It is almost here. And many of you are so anxious. You are so tired of the ways of life on earth, and suddenly, after eons of time, everything is going to shift. It's hard for you to wrap your minds around this and we understand. That is why we urge you to meditate and practice the various techniques shared in this book to help you feel your way into the change. The mind will have much more difficulty than the heart adapting to these new ideas. And, of course, the ego has the most to lose. Find your way through your beautiful hearts and that will prepare you best.

"What happens to the people who are not aware of what is actually occurring—those who are not living in fear, but just do not know where to turn?"

They are being well cared for as all the awakened ones are. They have a greater learning curve than you; yet it is not imperative that they know everything in order to make the shift. Being conscious and aware is the ideal, but they will still move with you into the new energies without this. These souls will be coached from the etheric realms to guide them through this process. No one that chooses the Light will be left behind, whatsoever.

"There are so many theories of what will actually happen when we shift. Will we still be on this actual earth or be above it?"

That is a question that makes people uneasy. Will your feet be on sure and steady ground, right? And the answer is yes. You will be standing on ground just as you are now, but it will be in another dimension and will require less density and this you will allow you to move with greater ease. So there will still be your physical earth, yet it will also be energetically less dense. You will also be above it, and I know that you may find this confusing, so let me explain. Think of it as an extra coating around the earth and this coating is of a higher vibration. You will still feel it's like earth, but it will be a mirror image set above it.

When you realize you are eternal beings, and you die and are reborn, sometimes on places other than earth, it is easier to accept. You are transforming into something new, but just without "dying" and having to lose your physical bodies.

*   *   *   *

So many of you are learning to watch your reactions to difficult situations. For some of you, there is no buffer and you react with words that can be biting. Or you take your anger out on your own being with anxiety and strain until it completely overwhelms you. Neither situation is healthy. My advice is to always stand in your power, breathe in Light, let it completely fill you, and deal with the situation appropriately. Always stand up for yourself, but tempered with kindness or, at least, neutrality. Don't automatically accuse another; just state how something affected you. Find ways to approach the situation, not with anger, but with fairness, striving to reach a mutual understanding. The other party may not understand or may cause additional stress. Stand strong and let us help you. Shine the Light all over you, your home, your automobile, everything and everywhere you are. Ask your angels to help you react appropriately, and to protect you.

"My way used to be to let things build inside, and I really do not like that feeling at all. Over time, I've learned to address things that need to be addressed, and sooner rather than later. When I come right out and deal with the situation, I can let it go instead of endlessly focusing on it over time. Every situation seems different. Sometimes, it feels as if I can just let it go, and other times the conflict calls for me to address it."

Your intuition will always guide one to the appropriate action or inaction. Sometimes, one is too tired or just wanting to ignore the intuitive signs or messages, but, when they really listen, the answer is always there. We know that life is not easy, yet when you understand that these conflicts are only helping you to grow, you can eventually ease into the learning so that the learning doesn't become more challenging due to ignoring what needs to be addressed.

"I've seen that so many times in my own life. When I ignore a lesson, it just comes back with other faces and other situations even more difficult, so I've learned to just deal and get it over with."

Time is precious to people. You lead busy lives, and time is greatly treasured. You will free up so much time to spend on what you wish, and not what you attract from your learning or from your karma. Anger and other negative emotions rob you of time and energy. Once you really get this, you will choose new ways to deal with situations.

"Sometimes, it seems that even when we feel we have learned a lesson, we are once again tested on the same lesson. Is this true?"

You are free to discover the truth of why anything happens. If you find this to be so, that you are repeating the lesson, ask us specifically why. We will always tell you or show you in some manner. Perhaps you thought you learned it, but hadn't achieved the best result. Or you may have learned an aspect of it, but not the full lesson itself. When the lesson is key to your growth, even if you successfully learned it, there are times you may be challenged again to really build on those correct behaviors. As you learn to accept lessons with grace, and strive to learn them sooner rather than later, you will find great rewards as a human and as a soul.

"As I mentioned before, I have issues with perfectionism in certain areas of my life. When I feel I haven't addressed my learning challenges perfectly, I can be really hard on myself."

You are not expected to be perfect, period. Many of you have issues with these tendencies to strive for perfection, and then feel as if you've failed when you cannot meet the lofty goals you set for yourselves. It's where your heart is at which is most important. Are you staying true to yourself as well as true to others? Are you coming from love or coming from anger and fear? What is in your heart is a good judge of whether you achieved the necessary lesson in a successful manner, and not your mind's judgment where perfectionism plays a role.

"That makes me breathe a sigh of relief. I've used the term 'good enough,' to help me fight my perfectionistic tendencies. So although my article, book, workshop, or interview may never be perfect, it can be good enough."

In that window to your soul, you can sense the perfection that lies within you. The closer you are connected to your soul, the closer you are to the perfection of you. Therefore, balance must be maintained between the desire for perfectionism and the ability to maintain it. You can strive to be the best you can be, and then have peace with the outcome achieved by doing your best. Then you accept and move on.

"Balance seems to be key in all areas of our lives."

That is so. And your intuition is always guiding you toward having balance, in addition to physical, mental, and emotional signals. Maintaining balance can come very naturally when you are tuned in to your inner world. One thing many of you are out of balance with is not having enough joy or play time.

"It's hard for many of us to find time for play when we're balancing so many more important things."

What you don't see is that when you bring play and joy into your life, in these moments it is very hard to feel stress and worry and you actually fuel your energy level. Overworking yourself can bring on negative energies such as resentment, frustration, and anger, in addition to exhaustion, which deplete you and you really don't have time for that either. You must have balance.

"I see your point. So many people are unhappy in their jobs, if they even have jobs with so much unemployment now, so, obviously, it is particularly important they find this balance."

As people connect with their souls, they will manifest work that pleases the depth of who they really are. They will attract what they need and desire to continue their growth. Imbalances are never desired by the soul; the soul desires balance and harmony. As you seek out balance and harmony, the Universe will comply to meet your demands.

"I cannot help but imagine that when we transition into the new age, every day will feel like Christmas."

Ask and ye shall receive. As you attain higher vibrations, you will manifest much easier than you do now. You will manifest the job that is in your highest interest or meet the person who you may have dreamed of your whole life. The possibilities grow exponentially when you are in a higher vibration. Do you wish for it to feel like Christmas every day? Ask and ye shall receive. Christmas is a state of being more than it is a holiday. What people get from Christmas are the feelings, the feelings of joy and surprise and comfort and love. It is always the feelings that people are after. Think about this. When you see a Christmas tree all lit up, what are you so joyful about? Is it really the tree itself, or is it the feelings of joy and celebration of the special time of the year? When you go buy all the decorations, the gifts, and the special foods—it is ultimately the feelings you desire, not the things themselves.

"Actually, this makes me realize that Christmas is a time when society *allows* us to live from our hearts, and that is very freeing for all of us who celebrate Christmas or a holiday similar to it. This is 'acceptable,' and we revel in it."

This is true. You see now that you can have this feeling every day, because, ultimately, your souls are driving you to lead from the heart; and one day you will consistently do so.

"What else do our souls drive us toward?"

To be in a constant state of gratitude. Many of you take things for granted and wonder why you are not manifesting that which you desire. Genuine heart-felt gratitude is your key to your desires. You do not have to go thanking every person, situation, and thing you encounter, although outward signs of appreciation are desirable when warranted. It is a state of mind to be in gratitude. It has no bounds. It breeds more to be grateful for. On the contrary, the lack of feeling gratitude creates the notion there is nothing to be grateful for so you keep getting nothing to be grateful for. Do you see how this works?

"Yes. Showing gratitude tells the Universe that one has so much to be grateful for. In return, the Universe continues to provide that which one keeps focusing on with such positive energy. For example, if I am grateful for a new friend, and appreciate all the wonderful qualities inherent in this friend, I will attract more friends with wonderful qualities. On the other hand, if a new friend comes into my life, and I don't appreciate who they are and take them for granted, the Universe will not give more of that which I am not focused on, or what I am not grateful for. We must focus on what makes us happy, and be in a state of gratitude. This makes perfect sense."

"I know that when I'm grateful for the synchronicities in my life, I attract more of them. Therefore, I receive more guidance, more validation, and more blessings simply because I'm focused on these gifts."

Think of synchronicity as God speaking to you. He speaks through signs and symbols, yet they often go unnoticed. Just as an angel's presence often goes unnoticed. But one day, synchronicities and angels and all the gifts of the Universe will become so very apparent that they will be impossible to ignore any longer. Then, magic and miracles are yours. It will be glorious.

"Angels and signs are the greatest gifts to behold. We need to awaken to these gifts. Since angels work through synchronicity, I feel that they are already making their nudges through signs so very apparent, so incredibly hard to ignore. People almost have to notice and, thus, awaken to the messages they are receiving. I imagine humanity awakening to these gifts in droves because of an upsurge in synchronicities. Now, that is something to really celebrate."

Do you know what else there will be to celebrate, and it is not too far in the future? It is the fact that you will all feel, as you transition into the new energy, that you have drunk from the fountain of youth. With your DNA changing, you will look as if years have been taken of your lives. So many of you in your 40s, 50s, and 60s have great issues with aging. You have frustration and anxiety over the natural process humans go through. The gift of youthfulness will be attained. Some of you are starting to feel the effects.

"Wow, you just threw that in there. Is it correct to assume that this will affect our physical appearance as well as our energy level?"

You will be affected in all ways. You will have youthful attitudes as well as more youthful bodies. You can partake in youthful activities, in addition to youthful thought processes, and that correlates with more open-mindedness! Neither you nor your neighbor will be complaining about age anymore. You will no longer feel you need to hide under makeup or your clothing choices. You will be well pleased.

"I adore how this book has naturally unfolded into a conversation. For a while, I wondered how this style would be received by readers versus having this book laid out by subject category where readers, like me, could jump out of order to the topic of their choice. But now I no longer wonder. I see the beauty of how these topics are subtly unfolding as we are in conversation, as we weave one conversation into the next. I like this subtle unfolding, and it feels right to me now. Is this an example of how we will change our ways, subtly and with ease?"

Many things will change subtly and over time, but there will also be those things that change in but a moment. There is nothing to fear as all is going according to plan. You only need to flow with the changes, and flow you will. Because you will have the wisdom and knowing that this has been what you have waited for. You have worked toward this for lifetimes. And when the shift finally occurs, you will flow with it naturally. You will be surprised by the grace and ease of living you will experience, as if you are just flowing with the river of life.

"What can prevent us from not going into fear regarding the shift?"

It is a choice to fear. Fear is an emotion that can arise when one is faced with the unknown. There is much unknown to you about the changes before you. However, many changes have already occurred, and those of you who have flowed with them understood what was going on behind the scenes. For instance, you witnessed the economic fall, but instead of going into fear, you celebrated. You understood this was necessary. And that is the way it is.

Look at everything that is occurring around you from a higher perspective and you will not hold fear. Look at all the Lightworkers sharing their messages of Light and see how that resonates in your heart. Look within and ask if you are tired of the darkness, the hatred, the deceit, and all the less than palatable ways of life on earth that you have endured for so long. Ask yourself if you are ready for this change. And, finally, look to your angels and the Universe's messages for comfort and guidance to show you the way to a new beginning.

Are you understanding the scope and magnitude of these changes? Life will never be the same, and that is for you to celebrate like you have never celebrated before. If these words make you shiver in fright, it is the process of change and the unknown that make you feel this way. I recommend that you start making little changes in your life and get used to the process of change. Learn to feel secure with change.

There is good news for those of you who fear change. When Heaven has descended on earth, you will no longer be triggered by your anti-change mindset. You will naturally embrace and accept your new life. Yes, acceptance will be a natural process as fear simply dissolves in the face of love.

"That sounds very evolved, that 'fear simply dissolves in the face of love.' We are all going through upheavals and trials that seem to be making us face our fears, temper our anger, and move toward love. Yet, we also need to stand up for ourselves at the same time, and not let others take advantage of us more peace-loving people."

That is among your more challenging lessons, to stay in the Light while dealing with the darkness. Once you learn these lessons, you can move on from them, and your growing Light will deflect the darkness. In every situation, as you endure these lessons, you have the choice to stand in the Light and stand proud and strong—or cower and join the darkness of anger and negativity. Just imagine the Light flowing through you, your angels with you supporting you, and allowing the Light and the angels to guide you.

"My friend recently got involved in a traffic accident. Signs were showing her that something was up just prior to the incident. Because of these warnings, she was cautious, and then the accident occurred. The other driver was clearly at fault, and my friend was quite angry and preparing to let loose with her emotions. When she saw the distress on his face, as he was so embarrassed and apologetic, she immediately calmed down before even saying a word to him."

Yes, and she made an excellent choice. Her accident was minor, but upsetting enough to cause alarm, and she learned to address the situation peacefully, rather than with anger. She tempered her anger and rather saw things from the other driver's perspective. And yes, she was warned that something was about to occur, and was on high alert. That was actually a gift. She had time to prepare herself.

"Signs can really lessen the shock. It seems that every time I'm about to be confronted with a challenge, synchronicity will warn me. I had an extremely difficult day last year, a day where I experienced one upset after another. I could not believe all that transpired during a single day. However, I was forewarned."

"That morning, as I backed my car out of the garage, an ambulance with its lights flashing went rushing behind me, and I had to stop abruptly. I intuitively felt that I was about to encounter some emergency; that I was 'backing into' some disaster. It prepared me for a day of great upset, and it helped me see things from a higher perspective. My way is to always bless all signs because I would rather have the warning than be shocked out of nowhere. By looking at it from a higher perspective, you realize, too, that the challenges are destined. There is peace in knowing that."

In the new energy, you will no longer experience shock. All will be known and understood. You will be telepathic and have a deep understanding of things, and peace will be the driving force. You will enjoy inner calm, instead of the frenzy and discord associated with some of the happenings of daily life. Synchronicity will be always present just as it is now, but it will be even more powerful and telling and mirroring of your lives and all that is around you. You will embark on new adventures with synchronicity as you explore your new way of living.

"This makes me very excited as I revel in the joys and magic of synchronicity. I am trying to imagine it being even more powerful than it already is. Would you say it will be more powerful simply because we will be more tuned in to it?"

You will understand it better, yes, but because it will be showing itself in a higher vibration, the signs will be keener and more defining. People will embrace rather than ignore signs. It will be part of the magic to be enjoyed by all.

"When you created those clouds in the sky that looked like jet planes, I realized then that people are going to see much more in the skies and will look to them for signs. People will be waking up to the possibilities that, yes, our angels can actually make cloud shapes. I believe that we, ourselves, affect clouds. I've even heard that one can make a cloud dissipate with their mind."

All you say is true. When you believe in yourselves, outside of conventional beliefs of what a human can or cannot do, you shall and will do things that would astound the nonbeliever. We say to you, keep looking to the skies for messages of love, in particular.

"When we traveled to New Mexico last year, we saw a perfectly shaped heart cloud. It ended up being an unexpectedly difficult trip for us, but the sighting helped us through. Soon after, we saw an inverted heart-shaped cloud, where the cloud defined the edges of a heart shape in the blue sky. Over time, we saw more of them, and then, suddenly, I started to see many pictures of heart-shaped clouds online."

That is exactly what I speak of. While you are going through such tumultuous changes on your earth, we are beaming love to you in so many ways. This is just one way.

"I feel the love from God when I view a sunrise or sunset. The colors in the sky seem more striking. Actually, everything in the sky seems to be more striking lately. We're seeing new cloud formations in areas that we're not used to seeing them, or the clouds are sometimes filled with color as if immersed in a rainbow. And, speaking of rainbows, the rainbows seem more prevalent and spectacular these days."

Yes, think of it in this way: your sky is reflecting the rising beauty coming from earth's inhabitants. As things change below, they change above, as well. Again, I say look up, perceive, and enjoy what the skies are telling you.

"Being a huge believer in and follower of synchronicity, I constantly watch for it now because signs are most definitely on the rise. Each day is filled with so many synchronicities that it seems they are so obvious that people are going to have to notice."

Signs will become increasingly difficult to ignore. This is true. There will also be a heightened awareness of all stimuli around you. Although you, Mary, and others like you have trained yourself to be this way, with the new energies people will naturally be more aware without trying. There will be many new inherent abilities that will surface, and this is one of them.

"What else will be new for us?"

You will hear much differently, and this sense will be used as a guiding force. Sound is indeed a guiding force, and you will embrace sounds from the Divine that will lead you, comfort you, and connect you to all that is.

"Do you mean this whistling sound that I hear in my head, what I call the 'spiritual sound' or 'God sound'? I know many others hear it too."

Indeed, all will hear this sound. Although you never knew what to do with this sound, but you will, and all shall utilize this Divine gift. All your senses will be broadened, in fact.

And your intuitive sense will become as clear as you can imagine. Tapping into your intuition will require no effort; it will just always be known. You will know just what to say, where to go, what to do, and how to interpret; all will naturally be known.

"Since we will be aware of who we really are—our very souls—it makes sense that as our souls talk to us through the heart, that this is really our intuition speaking to us directly. Will we still work with our angels for guidance, as well?"

Your angels will always be helping you. They can help you in ways that are outside of your understanding, and they can make miracles happen. Your relationships with the angels are not just about helping you to transition. You will be building these relationships to help you to continue to grow as evolving humans. It's a very creative process to work with your angels. You will gain much joy, and benefit in endless ways, by pushing the envelope in how you connect and work with your angels. And you can start now.

"Will we communicate in the same way as we do now, or will this evolve too?"

You will continue to speak from your mind or out loud, but the difference will be that you will telepathically or audibly hear your angels' responses in return. Yes, you will speak in conversation just as you and I are now, and you will understand with ease. Some of you already do this naturally, those of you who are psychically open. This will become an ability available to all, and as natural as your ability to walk or talk.

142

"This information gives me such joy. It makes me want to ask those who are not yet in communication with their angels if they would rather meet their new best friend now or later? Would they choose to go through their transition alone, or would they prefer immeasurable and often miraculous help to move forward with more ease? We all have this choice."

Yes, it is a choice, as you all have free will. Awareness helps people make decisions of their own choosing. Let these words serve as a vehicle for your awareness, and you can decide whether to test the waters or not. You are not judged. Your angels love you and celebrate you no matter what your choices are. No one is ever alone, and all of you are loved.

"One more thing about synchronicity. Many of us know that angels use synchronicity to give us messages. Personally speaking, this is a very significant way in which I feel the love from the angels. They remind us again and again of their love through signs, and especially on days that aren't so easy. They help us persevere, and they provide such magical blessings that, indeed, everything does seem possible."

The joy we feel when you recognize our blessings is immense. You bless us right back when you notice and feel gratitude for the blessings. Yes, anything is possible when you accept the gifts your angels desire to bestow with your permission. Just remember that you always need to keep an open mind and allow the space for seeds to grow the possibilities beyond your greatest dreams.

"Suddenly, everything is opening up. I recognize this with several friends and acquaintances, including myself. For one, we are receiving more magic and miracles, especially as more of us allow our angels to help; and we are finally able to step into our destined positions while remaining open to sudden and pleasantly surprising opportunities that seem to come out of nowhere. I was stuck for so many years myself. However, I now feel that the floodgates have opened and it is time to embrace the sudden flow in my life and work."

Face your lessons and struggles so that you keep the flow moving. If you ignore or don't achieve a lesson, this will hamper your flow. You cannot fully evolve without learning the basic life lessons you came in this life to conquer. Stay strong and watch your reactions. When you gain the wisdom and understanding your soul desired, you will continue to move forward. You will feel better about yourself and grow your self-love.

"What do you advise to those of us who don't love ourselves?"

As you peel away the parts of you that no longer serve you while growing closer to your soul and knowing who you are, you cannot help but find love there. Your soul is love, and it will reveal itself. The parts you haven't loved about yourself are those parts that blinded you to who you really are; whether it's the selfish, angry, or mean side of you that no longer belongs to the evolving human. When you remove the negative qualities, you will find love in its place.

"It's not always easy to be love when surrounded by so much negativity."

When you choose to not yell at your neighbor, and rather stand tall, shine Light, and seek a peaceful understanding, you will feel the love that is you. You are choosing love in that moment and that will affect you. If they don't comply, as they may still be embracing anger, you still have the choice to stand in the Light. You will connect with your heart before you react in anger at a future time, and then make the choice once again. That choice becomes easier and easier.

When you find yourself in a situation that calls for service to others, instead of just thinking about yourself and your needs, you give outwardly. The feelings gained from your gestures will fill you with love. You will feel rewarded for providing the service itself, and with no need for anything in return. Being in service takes you out of yourself and ends up creating more to love about you.

It is all the hatred, anger, rage, and dishonesty in the world that has reached such high levels that has forced you to choose love. As you honestly seek to transform the qualities that don't speak of love within yourselves, you convert them into love. You are changed and the world is changed. Go within to create the love you want in your world, in your own personal world, and you will achieve the results of your soul's greatest desire—to be love.

Others in your life who are choosing fear over love may try to keep you in their company. When they see you react in new ways, they may feel very uncomfortable. They have their own choice to learn from your behavior, or to try to keep you in fear. They may try to build up your anger and convince you to act otherwise. Hopefully, you will continue to choose the new way of being. That may or may not impact them. All you can do is shine the Light and be who you are. Always lead by example. Do not interfere with another's free will. Always stand proud. Always choose love, and when you forget your way, choose again.

Think of yourself as flowing in a river of love. There are rocks that represent hate and anger and other qualities that oppose love all the way down the river. You can continue your flow past the rocks and stay in the flow of love, or you can get stopped by the rocks and stop the flow. The further you continue down this river, you meet less and less rocks. They don't even matter at this point because

145

you are so cleansed and full of love that they couldn't affect your flow even if they tried. This is the way it shall be.

"What a beautiful visual. I got caught up with some rocks recently, and I eventually chose again. Someone would do something unkind out of the blue; it would test my reactions and I didn't always 'pass' the test. Once I realized what was going on from a higher perspective, I made better choices and reacted appropriately. So I like the thought that I just got back on the river of love. I know that these rocks get bigger and bigger, too hard to ignore, when we keep ignoring the lessons that we are presented with."

We can help you see the rocks, which could stand in your way, for what they truly are. And from there, you can make your choice.

As you flow on this river, many of you slow yourselves also because you are hung up on those thoughts that begin with the words, "If only...". "If only I waited another minute before getting into the car, I would not have been in that car accident." "If only I accepted that pay cut, I'd at least still have a job." "If only I went to college, I'd be happier in my work." These thoughts are wastes of your energy and emotions. There are no accidents, and there is reason behind everything.

When you accept this truth, you allow the flow of your life to occur without going back into the past and wishing for a different result. Reliving the past and wishing for a different result does not serve you. Making new choices that are in line with your heart's desire does serve you.

"Do we continue on this river in the new age?"

The river grows wider until it becomes an ocean, as each of your individual rivers feed into this ocean, and there you will be surrounded by love. The river is but a distant memory, and you are no longer touched by the negative influences. The ocean represents the oneness of all brought together in love and Light, and there you will have attained the peace your hearts desired for all your lifetimes.

"That sounds too good to be true, to actually live in peace."

That is because, as a human, you have never experienced this before. It's also hard to imagine when there is still so much strife and war and disarray all around you. You've had pockets of peace in various lifetimes, but this will be a peace never before known to you as a human being. For those of you who don't believe this is possible, go into your hearts and seek the pure truth. Check within and find out for yourselves if this will be your future reality. Your heart knows. As you connect with your heart and its wisdom, you make the transition easier. Your path to the ocean will be revealed in all its stunning glory.

"I am concerned that people, right after reading this, may check in with their hearts and will not immediately find the answer within."

That is because they don't have the confidence in their own inherent wisdom. I say to them: close your eyes, go within, and ask the wisdom that lies within your heart "Am I moving toward peace? Is the world moving toward peace?"

"How amazing. I never intentionally spoke to my heart before. And I felt this rush of energy and a feeling of celebration. 'Yes,' I heard. I feel like I just made a direct connection to my soul."

That you have. And so will those who genuinely speak to their hearts. Now ask your heart, what is it you desire?

"I received one word, 'Light!' My heart is the key to my soul. I understand this now. This is why we are to lead with our hearts. Because we will be living from whom we really are—our souls."

Yes, you not only know this now on a mental level, but you are feeling it as well. Speak to your hearts, dear ones! Celebrate the connection that will carry you through to the Golden Age. Make the effort to be consciously in touch with the deepest part of you, the most real and everlasting part of you. Your soul knows no bounds and is committed to guide you every step of the way through this glorious, yet, challenging journey. When you consciously connect, you allow for what may feel like an electrical connection within your being as if you are being turned on to a heightened set of possibilities. Open yourself to these possibilities. Feel the ecstasy of being connected with the real you. Trust your soul and the feelings that surface in your communication. Allow the communication to be two-way and not just coming from your soul. Your soul has waited for this. Communing with your soul is something that humans are not accustomed to. It's time to become accustomed, though. And when you do, it will be a grand reunion.

You are beginning to welcome your conscious aware-ness of your soul when you speak to the heart. So talk about anything and everything. Talk about what pleases you, what you are grateful for, and what problems you are addressing presently. When you speak to your soul, you not only receive an answer, but a heart-filled answer. An answer always doused in love and with wisdom you may have been unaware was ever within you. Don't look back, just be in the moment and share all you wish. Again, make the communication two-way. Expect an answer to your words because it is always there, and just speak now.

When you get in the habit of communicating with your soul, you will feel the weight of your problems lessen significantly, somewhat as if you are detaching from them. This is because your soul can help you see the higher

148

purpose of your problems, and that understanding releases the weight of them. Choose to work with your soul as if it is your best friend, and work through your issues. Create an understanding of self that will strengthen you and empower you to move forward with grace and determination.

"What do you say to those people who say they are talking to their hearts, but hear no response?"

I say to those of you who cannot hear your true self, you will hear your true voice when you have released the layers of that which no longer serves you. Is there a layer of guilt standing in the way? Are you filled with anger? Are you envious of someone else's life right now? These are all emotions that are masking your heart's voice, and you must surrender and release them.

Don't you see that the more you mirror whom you really are, the more conscious of a connection you will create? If your intentions are to be loving and forgiving, these are the highest qualities of self, and they mirror your soul's highest qualities. When you live in this state of unconditional love and forgiveness, you cannot help but become who you really are.

As you release the layers of you that no longer serve you, continue to talk to your heart. As you grow in your ability to connect with your heart, you will find your heart suddenly leading the way. Your heart will guide you to the greatest freedom you've ever known, as you find that love is all there is.

Life hands you all you need to embrace the growth your soul deems necessary. It creates the opportunities to see the Light in all situations and to master growth in all kinds of miraculous ways. When you understand this process, you see that everything is handed to you on a silver platter; but you often reject the platter, and want to ignore and make believe it is not there to help you grow. There is a missed opportunity, and these missed opportunities grow in magnitude until you cannot possibly ignore what's before you. You suddenly find the meaning in the lesson and you finally surrender to it. Do you see that you can make life incredibly more difficult than it has to be?

Learn to seek meaning in everything that happens to you. Catch the meaning when it is subtle and you do not have to put yourself through such unnecessary suffering. If you do not love your own self, for example, see it mirrored when someone says an unkind word or ignores you. Don't wait until someone spits in your face and screams at you. You will save yourself so much hardship when you face the truth of why things happen to you.

If you cannot curb your temptation to lie for your seeming self-benefit, see it mirrored to you when someone tells you little white lies that you know are not true. Don't wait until you suffer the effects of dishonesty that could cause you to lose someone or something important to you.

If you think you are not good enough, see it mirrored to you when you keep attracting others into your life who boast about their gifts and abilities, which in turn makes you feel lesser than, and you allow them to grow this misbelief. Don't wait until you attract an abusive person in your life who will try to solidify this misbelief in their violent or mean actions.

If you need to control your temper, see that need mirrored when another loses their temper with you, and you understand what it feels like. Don't wait until you find yourself in a more damaging situation from the effects of another's irritation with you that grows out of control.

When you abide by these lessons in the early stages with the awareness that you are learning it quickly, a peace will come over you. It will settle into your being, and you will feel the comfort received from tapping into your wisdom and taking the appropriate actions. This is the way now. Really take a look at what is going on in every given day and respond appropriately. Think of it as a dance and move with it. Make the appropriate steps and you will be graceful and sure. When you accept the dance with courage and understanding, with truth and honesty, your dance will be smooth and short-lived. If you move against the intended dance, you will be continuing it for a much longer time; and it will not be pleasurable, nor will it be too attractive.

"Throughout your explanation, I was thinking of Sherri Cortland's eye-opening book, *Windows of Opportunity.*[4] She encourages us to recognize these windows as they open, which can greatly accelerate our spiritual growth. Is there any other way we can be more aware of these lessons?"

Check in with your emotional state. What is making you feel unhappy, stressed, or conflicted in this moment? It is most likely that you are being faced with a lesson. Talk to your heart. Ask what it is that you may not be truly "seeing." And listen, just listen. There is always an answer. It may come through a feeling, words, or an image. There are many ways your heart can speak to you so it is important to just be open and without expectation. It may alert you to something that will occur in the near future; an opportunity to take advantage of, for example. It may review and reveal the deeper meaning of something in your past to describe how the lesson has been presented before. Just listen to your beautiful heart. It may shower you with so much information, at once, and will create a clear understanding in just an instant.

---

[4] Cortland, Sherri. *Windows of Opportunity.* Huntsville: Ozark Mountain Publishing, 2009.

"That is just the experience I had. I checked in with my heart about a concern, and I had this immediate and deeper understanding of this concern. It wasn't just words, but a combination of words with feelings and even visuals, in an instant of knowingness. Well, it's hard to explain."

This is the way to your most profound communication. Get in the habit of speaking to your heart, and you will never feel lost or confused. It will lead you.

"I just asked my heart what it wanted, and it said, 'freedom.'"

Yes, your heart wants freedom just as everyone's heart does. It wants the freedom to express itself, so that your heart, your soul is finally and truly heard. This voice, for most of you, has been stifled and ignored. Now is the time to honor your feelings and the source of your greatest wisdom. Now is the time to set your heart free.

Once you get in the habit of opening yourself to your heart, the process grows into a natural and constant flow of communication. It becomes effortless as you learn to connect and lead from your heart. The depth and vastness of information will flow through you, and you will feel the connection so deeply. You will feel the love flowing through you, the love that is you. And that will feel like opening the floodgates to a dam.

"When we feel such love, it softens everything else that is going on in our lives and the world: the chaos, the craziness, the constant shifting, and all the difficulties associated with it."

Love heals everything. Please do not take these words lightly. Love heals everything—all that you encounter on your path. Yes, the vibrational shifting and all the physical and emotional responses and challenges you are all experiencing are necessary and very real; but when you connect with your heart, ask love to heal you. Allow love to wash over your difficulties, symptoms, and struggles. As you do this for yourself, you do this for the world. As you connect with the love within you, you automatically help heal the world outside of you.

Yes, it is the connection to love that causes the flood-gates to break free. Imagine an explosion of love flooding you, your whole being, your family, your home, everything in your life. Let it happen. Allow it to happen. Do you see how the world will change? Do you see how love dissolves fear and other negativity? In the presence of love, a new way of being will evolve—and it will be grand.

"Will it not be harder to be around those who still feed off of fear?"

You will automatically attract like-minded people in your life who also feed on love. Once you're in the new ener-gy, love will always pervade. Until then, you will be less and less affected by the energy of fear and those who carry it within them. Your Light may affect them, but their fear will be less apt to affect you. The Light will win.

"The dark loses. So where does that leave those who carry great darkness within them, those who choose to remain in the darkness?"

They will not transition with the earth. They will continue to live in the environment conducive to their choice to remain living in fear and negativity. It is impor-tant, as much as possible, to stay focused on the Light, on love, on the shift, and what it will mean to you. That focus will make your transition and acceptance of change much easier. Do not worry about those who do not choose the new ways of living and being. Everyone has a choice and every-one is responsible only for themselves. Do not get caught up in the specifics as things continue to fall. The dramatic upheaval may cause some to choose differently, to finally see the Light. Others will not choose to change. Just as someone chooses a certain mate, a certain job, a certain philosophy to live by, it is not your job to get in the way of someone's choice. Leave it be. Stay focused on you.

As you connect with your souls, you lose attachments to thoughts of how things play out, and learn to accept things just as they are. Also, you are connecting to your inherent eternal wisdom which sees everything as perfection. And, thus, you will reside in a natural state of acceptance. You will no longer be swayed by what is being said on the television, by your neighbor, or even authority figures whom you used to put their beliefs over your own.

*   *   *   *

"Michael, last night before I went to sleep, I received the thought from you that I would have the ability to move into another dimension and become invisible to this dimension."

"After I received that message from you, I had a nightmare. Someone was running after me, and just when this person was about to catch up with me, I left the dimension we were in and was completely safe."

Many things are happening to you now so that you will write and share with others what is to come. Once you are able to physically access another dimension, you can slip back and forth while you still have consciousness in the dimension you presently live in. Of course, the real you is in many dimensions.

"Now that will take some getting used to, just thinking in those terms. It is so far out of the box. Life feels so different. Even from just a week ago. Is everyone feeling so different?"

Some are aware of it. Most are not. Life is already dif-

ferent, and it will become increasingly different. When people are in fear mode, they are not in touch with their feelings, except that they feel scared. How can one see the gifts of positive change when they are not allowing love in?

Can you feel the difference from how you felt last week, specifically? It is merely a surge in raising your love quotient. That changed everything. This is what happens when you open up to love. Love changes everything. Your upsets lessen, your patience grows, more joy fills you, more miracles appear, and you feel more peaceful.

Do you know what else is happening with you? That mental chatter you've had since you were a little girl, worrying and wondering about every little morsel of everything, is lessening. Many of you have this mental chatter that clouds your mind and makes it difficult for new thoughts to surface. The reduction of the chatter and the increase of refreshing new positive thoughts, instead of the constant rehashing of the old, will help you manifest what you desire, and not what you do not desire.

"This chatter has lessened, and, thus, as you say I am more peaceful. I have 'grown' my peace of mind."

There is a longing within each of you to connect with your higher self, your soul. You may not be aware of this, as it may lie deep within you, but it is so. When you consciously address this longing, you open a door that will never close again. Once you make this connection, your lives will turn right side up, as they have been upside down in many ways for most of you. That is only because you lost touch with your spirit, your spirit-uality. When you make contact with your spirit-uality, so much of the old you just slips away, as you become you.

Can you deny this? Can you ignore your spirit-uality? Do you want to continue down this same path of discon-nect, mostly because you do not like change? See change for what it is—freedom. When you get stuck in your ways and don't want to change something about yourself or your outer world, think freedom. Free yourself from the constraints and weights, which keep you from being who you really are.

Allow your spirit-uality to guide you to the easiest and most effortless course. It won't always be easy and effortless. Certain things must be endured. However, again, you can learn your lessons more quickly so they don't multiply and get more complicated and difficult. Choose the simpler path and create an easier shift for yourself. As you do so for you, you do so for the world. You help it shift, as well. This may be very hard for you to believe, but everything you are doing and thinking and feeling and saying is affecting the world. If only you could see what we see.

Never mind what anyone else thinks of you and your spirit-uality. It is a personal journey and a choice that distinguishes you as one who is choosing the Light, choosing love over fear. This will make some uncomfortable, but only because it makes them see things they don't like about themselves—it doesn't even have to do with you, only them—and they may or may not choose to change. Stay the course and shine your Light, yet do not force your beliefs on anyone. If they ask, you can share; and if they don't you just be, shining the light.

Clearly, you are becoming a new kind of human. One who breeds love, and not fear. You are concerned, perhaps, that this process is taking too much of a toll on you, but I promise you that as you shift and change, you will be rejuvenated and you will sustain the changes. You will not receive more than you can handle. Your bodies are designed to cooperate and to evolve. You need only go with the flow and surrender to this process. Fighting the process will impede it. Knowing you are all going through the same thing, knowing that you signed up to be part of this most momentous time in your earth's history, knowing that your soul is guiding you every step of the way—all these things can help you ease your way through the process.

There is one other thing that can benefit you as you shift, which we haven't yet discussed, and it is something humans have primarily ignored. That is, that you maintain groundedness. Consciously imagine bringing Light through your being and down into the earth. As you move your body, think "grounded" and maintain the strong connection to the earth. When you do this, you will experience less physical symptoms caused by your vibrational shifting.

When you feel these symptoms, you can ask your heart if the symptoms are those regarding the shift, or because of something else going on in your body that you must tend to. The most important thing you can do is to allow. If you fight, complain about, and focus on these uncomfortable sensations, you will prolong them. If you allow and accept they are a part of the process and actually a sign that you are progressing, they will flow through you and be short-lived.

*   *   *   *

"There seems to be a strange time warp or something like that going on. I may get a string of signs that something is going to happen that day, but then it doesn't happen, and you tell me that it will happen soon in the future. It's as if time is all mixed up right now."

You are right and you have always had great difficulty understanding the concepts of time, and the fact that time is an illusion. I tell you that you are moving into no time, or what some call "Now" time. This is what we have in

Heaven—no time. We aren't held by the illusions you have of time and space. So when we show you something that you will experience, it is in the "Now." And by telling you, you can expect it, create it, experience it, and then share it with readers. It has caused you recent frustration. However, you have held to your relentless faith and intense desire to understand, and we commend you. This is why you have been experiencing this, so that you would understand and write about it.

"So you're saying that as we create Heaven on earth, we also move into 'no time.'"

That is correct. What is important to understand right now is that you are in creation mode with all kinds of previews of what is to come as a guide to help set the expectations and, thus, create as you intend. You are receiving synchronicities that mirror not just what that very day is about, but also what will materialize "down the road."

"How will I know what is meant for the present time or when I should expect something to happen sometime in the future?"

You intuitively know what is a preview and what is immediate. You were just taking everything at face value, even though your intuition was telling you otherwise. One day, you will not see life as having a future, as there is only "Now," and it is eternal.

This is an exercise for you to learn to be comfortable with what you call this "time warp." As things shift, and as all of you grow your psychic senses, you may feel unsteady with your concepts regarding time. This is, ultimately, why spiritual teachers have taught again and again to live in the moment. For this practice is preparing you for a Heavenly life on earth.

"I guess time will tell... pardon the pun. I have been practicing relentless faith, because even though I was

158

confused, I was still very open to understanding. Although a part of me honestly wondered 'Now how is Michael going to explain this one?' and, of course, you did! I have always followed the guidance I've received, always with discernment that I'm hearing correctly, and it has never sent me down the wrong path. I truly give credit to the act of relentless faith because I always end up gaining the understanding I desire—and had I given up, I would have veered from my path."

*   *   *   *

Lo and behold, you are encountering a time of the end of sorrow. There will be no more sorrow and no more grieving. You will be in touch with all souls, and, therefore, you will no longer be disconnected from loved ones who have died, for example. You will be in full communication with any soul you wish to connect with. So the time of sorrow and grief is nearly over.

"Will we see them or just communicate telepathically?"

You will eventually be able to see them. It will be as if they had never left you, and you will communicate in many ways. You will speak as you would if they were still "alive," and you will create opportunities to gather and be together. But you can also speak telepathically when you are not together, and either of you are busy doing other things.

"I will ask a question that unexpectedly came to mind. Will we work together with our loved ones who have passed?"

You will have that choice. When you transition into living in your Heaven on earth existence, you must realize that it's not as if you will just sit there and be. The last thing we do here in Heaven is "rest in peace." We are active in all kinds of ways, just as you will be. There will be a world of things to do. And you will no longer experience the frustration, the stuck-ness, the poor timing, the inability to find your destined work—all of these cumbersome occurrences you may have experienced. You will manifest what you desire, and you will perform your purposeful work, of your choosing, with bliss and joy.

"Ever since I was a child, I've been uncomfortable with that phrase, 'rest in peace,' and your explanation validates how I've always felt about that. How will our work be different?"

Let me first explain what will stay the same. You will still be learning, and you will still be on your spiritual path. But what you will be learning will be as if you had been in elementary school on earth, and going for your advanced college degrees on your new earth. Rest assured that the learning will be filled with joy and excitement. The opportunities will show themselves and will delight you. You will carry your passions and your interests with you; that part of you will always be. They will coincide with the work you choose, or you'll discover within you the awakening of dormant or even completely new passions.

Even those of us in the angelic realms have our specialties. We each have our areas of strength and use them wisely. We are never in competition, as being connected to God gives us no reason to be. We help each of you according to who can best serve you in each of your unique situations. It will be no different for you in your service.

"Frankly, we are used to being in competition with each other, at work, in sports, etc."

When one is in competition, one is out to prove something. When you are aligned with your souls, there is nothing to prove to yourself or to anyone. You are this Divine spark of God, and there is nothing more you need to do other than just be who you are. Can you accept that finally you will all know you are good enough?

Competition is not desired when living in a higher vibration. There is no point to it. When you live in the third dimension, you may be unaware of the greatness that lies within you. Competition can bring that understanding forth, but it can also hinder it depending on your judgment regarding how well you perform. Once you see who you really are, there will be no desire to compete, nor feel envious or jealous of another. You will feel complete just as you are.

"I imagine this will make a lot of sports fans upset."

That is because they will be viewing this from a third dimensional mindset. Just as we spoke earlier that the need many have for coffee, alcohol, or other drugs will vanish, this is also hard to imagine from your present mindset. See from a higher perspective what it will be like. That you will feel such joy, peace, and bliss that your present needs will simply vanish.

"Truly, I can. In those moments I do experience the bliss, usually while in meditation, there is nothing to need or desire, period. Some people may be uncomfortable with this analogy, but at the point when one experiences an orgasm, I ask, does one need anything else right in that moment? When the veils between Heaven and earth have fully lifted, our paradigm for everything will change to a higher way of being, and we need to embrace it. Yes, the change will be so great, and so different from what we are used to. Yet once we are aware of it, and get a sampling of what it will be like, we will desire to embrace it whole-heartedly."

You have moved several times in recent years. You were following guidance even when it was extremely diffi-cult to do so, and put your family through the necessary changes, despite what other people thought.

"And it caused us to get used to change, to not be attached to anything. I do see how it prepared us to accept change and be at 'home' no matter where we are, although it happened for many reasons."

You are all being asked to learn to accept change and release attachments in all aspects of your lives, as it will make this process so much easier. Some are losing their homes and jobs and are forced to accept it. They are enduring extreme difficulties, and we are showering them with love and comfort. We want to help, with their permission.

"One of my favorites phrases I use is 'ease and effortlessness,' but sometimes it seems as if all the affirmations in the world will not get us out of our difficulties."

I will say again—the sooner you are aware of and address your lessons, the easier you move through them with the ease and effortlessness you speak of.

"Well, I feel we are all on this 'crash course' of life lessons right now. We're all quickly learning the lessons we may have ignored time and time again, because now they are right in our faces, one right after another."

This is true. Everything is quickening now to prepare you for this shift. It is opening the gateway to a spiritually led life, the kind of life most of you have strayed from. You are returning to your spiritual roots, which is your natural state. Society no longer drives you; you drive you.

"We need to un-brainwash ourselves; that's the way I see it. And, at the same time, empower ourselves. So many of us are unaware of the power we have. We are unaware that we have the power to create and the power to change, and we don't need anyone telling us what to do or what to think. The only way is within, especially now, so that we don't allow the fear out there to grip us again and again."

Once you make this shift, it becomes natural, and you become in charge of you. Imagine waking up in the morning and making your decisions, one by one, according to your own inner voice. Are you going to eat that breakfast because society told you this is what you should have, or because your body told you this is what your body needs right now? Are you going to drive to work with thoughts of worry and concern over what the day will bring, or with a smile on your face knowing that you are creating the day yourself; and if difficult challenges surface, will you meet them head on with courage and determination? Are you going to have lunch with coworkers who drain you with gossip and fear-based talk, or will you make a different life-enhancing choice? Yes, it is all about choices and using your inner voice to guide you through your day.

What actions enhance your life? Would it be a smile or a frown, laughter or anger, success or failure, peace or upset? You would think I'm stating the obvious, but how much of your energy and thoughts are focused on the negative qualities and actions such as those mentioned? Most people most of the time concentrate on the negative, and, thus, create more negativity. When you live from your heart, you concentrate on love, joy, laughter, and life-giving actions. It is your natural state. It is what we want for you, but it is your choice.

"When I connect with my heart, I immediately connect with the joy and peace that is there. I feel elevated from my third dimensional self and do see things differently from this place. I am starting to really understand this."

Your heart knows all, and in that place you will find the wisdom you have always desired. You do see things from a higher dimension when you connect to your heart, and this very connection will help you significantly in your transition. Not just for yourself, but as you connect with

others from this heart space—it elevates all of those involv-
ed. You can even imagine this as you communicate with
others, that the thoughts and words are coming from your
heart.

You are starting to notice that you are in commun-
ication with others even when you're not, in your reality,
speaking with them. A friend just wrote you today saying
that she "feels your energy so much lately," as this friend is
an energetically sensitive and highly intuitive being. She
said she feels like she is "talking to you." In your reality,
you haven't yet had an actual conversation, as she lives
half way around the world, and you only converse through
your computers. But, in truth, you are in communication
through your souls.

"I do feel that, as I know that Talia and I are in the
same 'spiritual family,' and we were destined to meet; as
all of us are meeting members of our spiritual family. Now
more than ever, I consider this among my greatest gifts—
to connect with my soul sisters and brothers."

You, too, have been feeling such connection with her as
well as with others close to your heart, even when not in
verbal or physical contact. That feeling is a result of your
hearts being in connection. You are communicating soul to
soul.

"That is so beautiful. When I have thoughts of
someone that keep popping up, I'm feeling they are
thinking of me as well. Yet, you're saying that it's really
our souls via that heart connection."

As you get used to this, you will more purposefully
connect soul-to-soul. You will receive telepathic under-
standings from the other. You can even test this. When you
get a "hit" about someone, let them know and see if your
reception was correct.

"Some readers may be concerned with this news,

wondering what will happen to their privacy. This thought has crossed my mind, as well."

When you become more of who you really are, privacy "goes out the window." I realize this will be hard for many to accept, but there is more to this than may meet the eye. Your positive qualities shine as your negative qualities wane. There will be nothing to hide. The new energies will not tolerate dishonesty, anyways, so truthfulness will prevail. Shame, guilt, regret, and such will dissolve as you step into the magnificence of who you are. The past will not affect you anymore. Can you imagine how this will be? For those in the Heavenly realms, there is nothing to hide. All is known as we are all connected, just as you are part of this whole. Your misbelief that you are separate from each other and the Source of all that is has created the disconnect. However, when you connect with who you are, you connect with all that is, as well.

"Michael, I took a break from writing just now, as you know. I saw online that there is a 'Oneness Day Petition' (at www.humanitysteam.org) asking for 'signatures to appeal to the United Nations to declare a global Oneness Day,' to symbolize moving 'toward a New Spirituality, a new humanity, a new earth.' Oh, how the world is changing! And you synchronistically keep showing me things that mirror what I'm channeling from you. I am so grateful."

It is for you, and it is also for your readers, to understand how validating synchronicity can be. As you absorb the new energies more and more, you will experience this phenomenon much more often. You will flow with the universal flow of synchronicity. As you make a choice or are introduced to a new thought, synchronicity immediately steps in and mirrors it. This is another reason it is important to tap your intuition. Your intuition told you to take a break and told you just where to go so you would experience the synchronicity.

"This has happened so many times while writing this book. You'll say something that is a completely new idea for me, and then synchronicity will soon, if not immediately, find me and mirror it in some way. Sometimes it's your whispers guiding me toward the validation. I do feel the speeding up of synchronicity. I also feel there is an ebb and flow to it, as there is to all things. But, overall, it is ever more present in our lives."

It all has to do with the energies, as the higher energies create more awe-inspiring synchronicities, as well as a rise in their occurrences. The gift of synchronicity, when noticed and pursued, gives people more strength to endure the challenges before them. It is not difficult to understand synchronicity; it is merely a new way of looking at life. When you embrace it, you work with the flow of the Universe and create harmony in your life.

"Harmony, yes... I don't believe I ever used this word in regard to synchronicity, but I see now that harmony is what is created. You realize that all that is occurring is in perfect flow with the Universe, and, thus, creates a harmonious existence within no matter what is going on outside of us."

"I imagine that synchronicity will be so prevalent in peoples' lives that those who deemed it as coincidence over and over again will finally rethink their beliefs."

Synchronicity will become impossible to ignore. You wrote your first book giving people a "heads up" so they could start paying attention, if they haven't already. They can choose to ignore it when it comes in softly and gently. Yet, when it appears with great intensity, they will face the reality of it. And, as you know, once you become aware, there is no going back to the old ways of believing that

166

everything in life is random. It will change their paradigm of belief of what kind of Universe they really live in. It is a beautiful Universe that is magical and exact, and one that breeds creative beings.

Yes, you are all creative beings, as you are in the act of creating every moment of your lives. Your choice is whether you create consciously or unconsciously. You empower yourself to create as you consciously desire, or you can lie victim to creating from unconscious misbeliefs, pain, and suffering from your past. When Heaven is created on earth, you will no longer create from your unconscious mind.

"That is huge news. So all the misbeliefs we hold onto about ourselves—from our childhoods, most especially, and even baggage from our past lives that also runs us like computer software until we can release it—will no longer affect us? Regarding those things we haven't yet healed, will they just be erased?"

At the energetic vibrations you will attain, the paradigm for how you create will change. You will create from your soul's desires, not from the past experiences that created beliefs—often misbeliefs—that tied you to your past. Imagine that being erased, and there will be a newly formed connection to your soul. And from there, you will communicate and create the highest dream of who you are. You will manifest your conscious desires without the blockages and stuck-ness you've experienced so. Imagine how magical this new way of being will show itself.

Embrace the magic, and desire the ease and freedom. Many of you are starting to experience this now, as you're already tapping into these higher vibrations, but it will only increase as humanity moves closer to the shift in the collective vibrations.

"Never before have things just 'fallen into my lap,' as they are now in many ways, especially with regard to my work. There are people who have come into my life and just do amazingly supportive things for me. Now, I admit I have never been one who receives very well. I am better at giving, yet I am learning something new here. I am learning to have that balance. I desire and embrace the magic and the higher vibrations, and am overjoyed that we're now getting previews of what is to come."

They are previews, but the magnitude of just how magical life will be may even extend beyond your imagination. You all are so used to struggle. Can you open your minds to what a more Heavenly existence will look like? Go outside of the box of what you presently live in and imagine what life will be like. Dare to dream the highest dream for yourself. Let Heaven begin to shower you with all you have ever desired and more. Allow for the unknown and unexpected, and breathe in all the possibilities that are before you.

"When I imagine what it will be like, my greatest joy is the peace we will feel. More than anything, peace stands out to me."

Most of you are tired and weary from the wars, the arguments, the lies, and deception. You crave peace, but many have not imagined it is possible to live on earth with peace. I tell you it is vital for each of you to hold peace within, no matter what is going on outside of you. Concentrate on moving toward peace in all situations.

That does not mean you let people walk all over you— absolutely not! If a situation arises that disturbs your peace, you stand tall and stand up for yourself. But anger does not rule your behavior, within or outside of you. You buffer any instinct to yell and criticize. You allow the Light to protect you and communicate in a constructive way. You find a peaceful resolution. Ask your angels to help you through.

Again, pay attention within. Even though you may have maintained peace outwardly, check within to make sure that is mirrored there, as well. Always live from the inside out, and not the other way around.

"Can't we be hiding our anger even from ourselves? How can we be sure that there is truly peace within?"

If a situation continues or returns, you are either still being tested, or there is more for you to face. Think of the person who has "done you wrong." Tune inside and ask yourself, "What do I feel about him/her?" If the feeling is neutral—if there is no emotional charge—you have done the work. Finally, you can "throw love" on the situation, and heal the situation with love. Then release it.

"You make it sound easy, but it is not so easy sometimes."

The path to spiritual growth is not designed to be easy, although certain aspects make it easier, such as the knowingness that you have God's love. You have your angels' help, if you so choose. And you have many spiritual tools. Awareness is always the first step. When you are aware of what is really occurring in all aspects of your lives, and utilize your wisdom to grow from it, this is the key to easing into new levels of your spiritual growth.

You can call on me or on any being in the higher realms when you cannot find your way to peace; we will help pave the way for you. We can work with you and the "opposing" side to find your way to peace. You may say, "Life is not fair," and I say, always see things from a higher perspective and that viewpoint will bring peace into your heart. Call on us and we will help you understand and make new choices that will ultimately allow you to just be love.

"Well, you really helped me to see how much I was focusing on a negative situation recently. I'm now able to see how obsessive my thoughts were regarding it. Once I became aware, I was able to truly let it go, but, yes, it is definitely the act of being aware that is making the difference. Also, I listened to my heart."

Your heart will guide you when you really listen. And remember, you can have a conversation with your heart just as we are having a conversation. You may say, "This is crazy to have a conversation with my heart." Is it really? Would you rather have a deep conversation with your heart that provides the love and wisdom to help you through, or go it alone? Or rely first on others, such as well-intentioned friends, who will advise you, but may not understand your path? Will it hurt you to try a new way? Your ways of being haven't worked out so well on your planet. People must be open to new avenues to break free from what no longer works.

"But you're not saying our friends cannot help us, right?"

Sometimes, your friends are the vehicles that help you get to that "light bulb moment." We often whisper to your friends when you yourself don't hear our whispers. Always be open to how you receive your help and wisdom. Always enjoy the comfort and help that a true friend provides, of course! What I am saying is that, ultimately, your way to growth is to first go within. Don't keep reaching outside yourself to fix your issues; first go within. And from there, you will always, always find your way.

"By the way, a few days ago you said we could 'test' our telepathic abilities. I didn't share that with anyone. However, this morning, I had this strong urge to take a more scenic route as I dropped my daughter off at school. When we arrived, my daughter said she couldn't believe I drove that way because she said she was telepathically asking me to drive that route without actually saying a word to me. My very tuned in daughter tested her telepathic skills without knowing you suggested it, and I was able to receive."

She heard my whispers, and she is so beautifully receptive; she picked right up on it. May this inspire you and your readers to communicate telepathically in a proactive manner. This must only be used for the highest good of all involved. This is not meant to be used as a manipulative tool because if it is used in this way it will backfire completely. You can send love with your thoughts, imagining it coming from your heart. You can send positive and inspiring wishes to someone. Imagine all the ways you can communicate in this manner.

"Once we experienced this telepathic transmission, I shared with my daughter what you taught me. Then, tonight my daughter emailed someone for help with something. This person responded saying, 'It's weird that I checked my email tonight. I usually just check it in the morning at work. You must have sent me a mental message!' We were laughing over this one. Certainly, this further opened my daughter's mind to her ability to send thoughts telepathically. We even played a game where one of us would think of a food, and we'd think it, feel it, use all our senses to describe it, and mentally 'send it' to the other person. She guessed 'asparagus' and she was right! But other times, we weren't right. It seemed like we were making it difficult."

When you are communicating telepathically, it is an effortless process. It will be as natural as picking up the phone to call someone, but it will be instantaneous communication. When you receive messages from me, they are often in thought groups, and you manage to decipher the message into words. This is how telepathic communications will work. In an instant you will have the full understanding.

"Sometimes, I do hear the individual words from you, and other times it seems to be this basic understanding of what the message is, and then the words just follow. It's difficult to explain. It just happens."

As telepathy just happens. Again, it is an instant-aneous understanding of what is being communicated. It actually affords a more pure understanding for it feels more complete.

"Because words can oftentimes be incomplete, right?"

Telepathic communications provide a thorough under-standing of what is being communicated. It provides the combination of thoughts, intentions, and feelings as well. Words are an attempt to fully describe the thoughts, but may communicate little more. For instance, when someone says, "I love you" to another, the words are powerful. But when "I love you" is sent telepathically the message is more complete with a purer understanding of what that person feels and knows. Try sending, "I love you" to another without saying the words.

"I am sending an 'I love you' to my friend Clare, and also telepathically asking her to contact me. We usually communicate often, but I haven't heard from her too much lately."

(Almost two hours later Clare called me. I told her that nearly two hours prior I had telepathically asked her to call me, and she said she *was* thinking of me then, yet it was too early to call.)

"I just had the realization that when I speak to my angels, I almost always do so from my mind because I know they hear me. As we evolve this ability, I can start communicating in the same way with my fellow humans. This takes adjusting to a new way of communicating. So is that why it's a good idea to practice it?"

When you fully shift, you will automatically have this ability; and I say again, it will be effortless. But for you wonderfully curious souls, I say start practicing so you can see what it is like. You will be amazed, and it will excite you as you get a taste of what is to come.

Open your mind to the possibilities this will offer. Imagine the benefits of what telepathic communications will bring. I don't think, Mary, that you have really considered this. Can you imagine what it will be like when you witness the sending and receiving of purer communications? You have disliked misunderstandings since you were young. It has frustrated you because you have suffered from so many misunderstandings, and they really weighed on your heart.

"Misunderstandings have always been so frustrating to me. There were times I felt that no matter what I said the other would not truly understand it. They would make their own judgments or come to their own conclusions."

Misunderstandings vanish when you become telepathic. Imagine a world where "voices" are truly heard. So often, peoples' present misunderstandings lead to grosser misunderstandings, and suddenly you have a big problem that would never had manifested if there was clearer understanding to begin with. In the new energies, there will be understanding the first time around.

I heard your thought, and yes, there will be less drama! There will be less conflict! Can you imagine that? There will be such peace in your hearts that you will have no desire to kick up dust.

"It sounds like a perfect world. Will it be perfect?"

You will still be learning, and in order to learn you will still have challenges. But when I say challenges, it will not even remotely resemble anything like the challenges you have had in the past, or now have before you. You will learn in a more cooperative and loving world. A world that is peaceful and nurturing. A world that is magical and loving. You will be busy. You will have work. You will have your families to nurture and to love. You will have plenty to do and much to enjoy. You will never feel bored, and you will always find fulfillment in all you provide for yourself and for others.

People who love drama, focus on drama, and, thus, attract drama, are bored with life. This is why I point out that drama will wane, and yet you won't be bored. Rather, you will be fulfilled and content and not seeking things that don't serve you.

"This makes perfect sense. Honestly, the times I feel least bored are always when I feel most connected spiritually. When we are connected on a spiritual level, there is nothing to be bored about. Not only because new abilities and understandings are coming through, but because of the access to love and bliss."

You are getting closer to understanding the total picture. This book is an unfolding, and I know it has frustrated you to not compartmentalize this book for the sake of the readers. You wanted chapters that would describe all the different phases of change and what readers could expect, and how to heal their past, and on and on.

"This is true because that's how I like reading and writing a book myself, organized into chapters with specific titles describing what is to be expected within it."

Of course, the way this book has played out is very intentional. It is meant to be read as an unfolding. For one, there are those, like you, who sometimes jump around in a book. This book is not meant to be read in this way. It is meant to be read as it was channeled, to slowly and purposefully present the material in a way that helps readers to see the bigger picture. We thank you for allowing the process to unfold as intended, even though it is against your desires.

"Actually, this gives me the validation of knowing that I'm leaving me out of it!"

You are honored for your trust in the process. And now, we move to the next topic in the process of the unveiling...

Your level of intelligence. As you continue to raise your vibration, you will be accessing higher levels of intelligence within you, intelligence that has lain dormant within you for many lifetimes. You will access information through your heart, and you will discern and utilize this information for higher understandings of how the world works. This will empower all to seek within and lessen the need to look outside oneself for all the answers.

"We're all going to be smarter?"

Smarter and wiser. When you tap into the wisdom in your heart, you move forward with sure footedness. You will have so many tools to make purposeful decisions and choices. On present-day earth, it often takes a long time to make real change happen, certainly with your political processes. But imagine "cutting to the chase" and seeing the light on humanity's issues, as well as personal ones, and making grand change where necessary.

"That is music to the ears. Here in America, people are literally dying for change, whether it's because they cannot get health care when they desperately need it most, or they are suffering the effects of dangerous foods, and on and on. The wars continue to be fought around the world, no matter how many lives are lost, no matter how many are threatened and ruined, and no matter how many are sickened by it and crave peace. And change in many ways seems to be arriving at a snail's pace, no matter what is going on right before our eyes. I know this

175

will change, but it cannot change soon enough."

These institutions and forces that are causing unrest and injustices among the masses are crumbling. We are deeply saddened over every loss and hardship endured. As difficult as it may be to accept or understand, on a soul level all who endure all types of hardships came into this lifetime with the agreement they would endure them, as they are a significant part of shifting this earth into a Heavenly earth. Those souls who perish will return to a better world and in conditions that will not at all resemble the horror they left.

*   *   *   *

Life sometimes seems to have lost its meaning as you embark on the greatest change ever to occur in your lifetimes. This is a temporary feeling. When witnessing the worst of humanity, your beliefs and expectations change and you feel helpless. Again, this will not last for long. You will take control of your lives and empower yourselves to enact great change. The Universe will support you fully. You are witnessing the worst of humanity in order to experience and know the best of humanity. When you have those moments of disconnect and, perhaps, helplessness, call on us to help you through. We will help you stay strong as the captain of your own ship as you sail through the rocky seas of these challenging times.

"This is exactly what I feel at times—disconnect. It seems to come in waves and makes me feel very vulnerable, and then suddenly I reconnect and feel strong again."

The ride is still rocky, but it will not remain as such. You will continue to go through this pattern of experiencing these symptoms of the shift until the waves lessen into eventual stillness.

"What about the people who are unaware of what is going on?"

There will be those whose hearts will lead them to the same destination, but they won't be conscious of the process. It is another pathway to the same place. For those who want the conscious experience of evolution, this book is written for.

You are weaving your way toward evolution either way, but when you do so consciously, it will feel more peaceful because you will have the understanding and wisdom behind all that is occurring.

When one is aware of their evolutional path and is engaged in it, they hold less fear when they experience change on a personal or global level. Can you imagine feeling all these symptoms from the vibrational changes and not understanding their source?

"The understanding of their source is what gets me through these times. I cannot imagine not being aware. I think about this often. How are people who don't really know what is going on—who don't know that we are evolving—coping with everything? It has to be scary as they try to understand what is occurring within and all around them."

This is why the Lightworkers are doing their work to raise as much awareness as possible to ease others' transitions. It is not easy work, and they must hold true to their mission while some may discredit them. My advice to Lightworkers is to allow the Light to protect you. And, of course, work with your angels, as they can protect you as well. Many Lightworkers have lost sight of the angelic help that is waiting to serve them. It is not too late to begin connecting with your angels. You can start right now, and share your practice with those wanting the same.

"What else can we Lightworkers do, that we aren't yet doing?"

Be the example; don't just talk about it or write about it. "Be love" in everything you do and say. This will give integrity to your message. When you fall off the wagon, so to speak, share your experiences honestly as you get back on. You are human. We only expect you to walk your talk; knowing that intention, not perfection, is the desired effect. Do not hide what is in your heart. Be true to who you really are.

When others witness your humanness coupled with your spiritual strength, it will inspire them to pursue the path, forgiving themselves when they sway from it. When they see the joy in your face and in your message, no matter what is going on around you, they will want the same for themselves.

*   *   *   *

"This morning, I woke with the sound of ice falling to the floor. The time as I write this right now is 4:44 a.m., the number combination known to mean the angels' sign of the power of God's love. Usually you wake me with the sound of a doorbell. Why this?"

You took a needed break for a few days as you went on your trip. I chose to wake you with a new sound to really get your attention. You believe that water spilling on yourself is a sign of increasing abundance. I'm also showing you that with the ice falling, you're going to get a huge surprise of increasing abundance. The abundance will be coming with a force.

"Well I certainly like that. It did make me laugh because last night when I used the ice dispenser, the ice machine was overfilling, and ice was falling to the floor.

So the sound was fresh in my mind, you might say."

"I felt like there might be more to this, so I'm glad I asked. Actually, I think you were whispering to me to ask you about it, and I have to say I was pleasantly surprised by the answer. Of course, abundance takes many forms, not just in the financial arena. You just introduced to me a new synchronistic meaning—abundance coming with a force."

"I've also had many synchronicities with money trucks. On one February morning this year of 2010, I was confronted with a huge and unexpected financial loss. Just after learning what I was faced with, I went to Vitamin Cottage, a local health food store. I paid for and picked up my groceries, walked a few steps, and nearly ran into a man who drives a money truck. I intuitively felt that this was a sign that I not worry about my finances. I proceeded to see the number combination '888' on license plates several times, especially over the next few days. And of course, numerologically speaking, 8 is the money number."

"Days later, my daughter and I were walking out of Kohl's department store, and a money truck stopped at a stop sign started to drive forward, suddenly saw us, and then braked abruptly—again nearly 'running into money.'"

"In late April, I went to Whole Foods, and yet again on my way out of the store, I literally almost ran into another man who drives a money truck!"

"Two days later, I went to pick up a few things back at Vitamin Cottage and as I was placing the groceries onto the checkout counter, I heard a man say, 'This is my first time here. Where do I go?' Had he not said anything, I would not have looked up, as I was busy with my groceries. Since I thought it was strange what he said, I turned my head only to find it was yet another man who drives a money truck."

"Now, it is not normal for me to literally (nearly) run into people. In fact, it is extremely rare. I also rarely see these men who drive money trucks, up close. Suddenly, I'm not only seeing them, but also nearly running into them. These signs have helped me relax about the illusion of my financial 'woes.'"

You're running into money. Abundance will come with a force. These are all wonderful synchronicities for you to enjoy and trust in. Let me take it one step further. You, Mary, are an example for all of you reading these words that these promises delivered through synchronicities can be yours, as well. Mary's intention is that she has enough money to sustain herself and her family because she has no question of her mission in life, which is to be a Lightworker and to help humans evolve. For years, she has made little money doing so, and yet she is indeed attracting the means to continue her work. She doesn't know how the money will come in to sustain her and her family, but she is trusting and putting all her focus on her mission. You can attract the same for you.

"I have not yet seen the financial abundance that the Universe keeps previewing for me, and the signs didn't stop at the grocery store. One morning in May, I was guided to do something that would significantly add to the sudden piling up of expenses I was incurring throughout the month. When driving an hour or so later, and as I approached a road roundabout, I synchronistically met up with a money truck. I drove about a half mile further, and just as I was turning onto a road, the oncoming car turning in immediately after me had a license plate with the numbers '888.' Just as I completed the turn, eight Canadian geese flew right over my car. Although I was

180

already quite convinced that I needed to follow guidance, this was a beautiful set of validations from the Universe."

You've been learning a new lesson. Sometimes, common sense would tell you one thing, yet an overriding feeling in your heart tells you to persevere with courage and determination on a certain decision, such as spending money on something that common sense would tell you not to when the world's troubled economy is causing most people to "tighten their belts." Your heart is leading you to make seemingly nonsensical decisions for perhaps unknown reasons yet to unfold.

"Exactly. My inner wisdom was suddenly countering what my common sense would normally dictate. So many times I've started a sentence directed to my friends: 'This is going to sound crazy, but...' and they understand that I'm guided to do so, even against what common sense would direct me to do. Although in my heart I trust my decisions, because I discern everything to death and make sure I'm hearing right, it's nice when others understand it. Nothing remotely compares to validation from the Universe though. I've learned to seek validation from the Universe, and quell the desire to seek it from others."

Mary, you often wonder how this book will affect others, and I tell you again that it is everyone's individual responsibility how they utilize these lessons. The ultimate guidance for each of you readers is your own guidance. What you glean from this book can produce a new way of seeing, but it is each of your own personal responsibility to make your own interpretations and decisions.

"Getting back to your message from yesterday, as I went off on quite a tangent this morning, you said that Lightworkers can be the example?"

This is true. It shows others that they can choose to find their own path to the Light. Only you can decide what is an appropriate path for you. You may be swayed off your path by others who think their way is better. You may be enticed by the messages others are putting forth. Someone may claim his or her way is the quickest and easiest choice. The answer is always within. If you go within, you cannot ever go wrong. You must know and learn to trust this.

So be examples by shining the light, but each person must find their way and acknowledge their truth by connecting with their hearts. Some of you who are reading this still have not tried to connect with your hearts. You think it's too difficult, too strange, or even just a meaning-less exercise. You will be surprised by what this connection will provide when you simply just talk to your heart.

Talking to your heart will fill you with great peace. You will tune into the love that is who you are. When you have a problem, just talk to your heart and allow for the answer. You may think it is your imagination that is answering. Do not let that stop you. Stay with it. The answers are always there. Just allow.

What motivates one to do anything? The soul. When you consciously work with the soul, through the heart, do you see how you can achieve your purpose? Do you see how you can work through your issues in a clear and direct way? Do you understand why certain people and events are appearing in your life? You have much to gain when you connect with your soul in a conscious, rather than uncon-scious way.

"I lived most of my life unconsciously. When my spiritual path began in 1994, I made the switch to living consciously, and I can tell you that my life has improved so significantly since I made that choice. It is the deeper understanding that I most treasure. The understanding that this Universe serves us just what we attract, and we can learn to attract what we truly desire rather than accept what we unconsciously bring forth in our lives, which is often much less desirable."

In the new energy, you will be intrinsically connected to who you really are that you will naturally attract everything you desire without effort. Do not wait until then to start understanding and working with this process. By learning it in lower dimensions, you are gaining spiritual growth. It is as if you're going from grade school to high school in an instant without gaining from the benefit of all the learning in between.

You, Mary, have chosen to live as a human with spiritual understanding, to find God and learn who you really are while in this lower dimension. When you do this, you gain what is most treasured in an earthly incarnation... experience. You experience being a physical being in a physical world with a nonphysical and Heavenly world to tap into. You observed others who had no desire to understand their true home while living on earth, yet it never swayed you from your own path. You chose to live from the inside out.

Many of you have made this choice, as well, and understand the benefit of being in, but not of, the third dimensional world. In the new world, you will be in, and of it; embracing it as your home, as a member and not a visitor. Your days of feeling like a visitor are almost over. Soon you will be home.

"That is music to my ears. It is hard to wrap the mind around the idea of living in a physical world that is also a Heavenly one."

Nonetheless, it is where you are heading. When you stay connected through the process of change, you will endure the ripples, the difficulties, with great acceptance. When you lose connection, or if you never sought this kind of connection in the first place, the bumps in the road will be felt much more abruptly and significantly. It behooves you ever so much to maintain connection at all times.

"When I am disconnected, everything seems to fall apart for me. I've learned time and time again that talking to my angels, watching for synchronicity, meditating, reading spiritual material, etc., always gets me back on track."

Another way to stay on track is to embrace each other throughout this process. Seek out like-minded people who desire peace in their lives, as well. When two or more are gathered, powerful things happen. Even more so now, in the shifting energies. You don't give your power to anyone, but share in your positive energies, and this creates a force, a mechanism to clear the way toward change.

"When going through such great changes, we don't want to feel alone now, of all times. I have such peace in knowing that my angels are with me. I wake most every morning physically feeling their presence. When I have connection with like-minded people, it fulfills me in a different, yet still powerful way."

Because you will become increasingly telepathic, you can help each other in more constructive ways. You can view each other from a more honest and clear perspective because the telepathy reveals more direct information about each other.

"We often hide our feelings even from those we trust and love, perhaps to not burden another. Or we have trouble getting our feelings across. So I can see how with telepathic transference, the truth will be heard and understood."

Let the truth be told, no matter what it is, because truth is essential in the new energy. A lie cannot survive in the new energy. All is known, and truth is honored and celebrated. You see what lies have created in the world you

184

are leaving, and lies should not be missed. Here in the Heavenly realms, nothing is hidden, as all is transparent. Seek the truth now in all you say and do, and this change will come with ease.

"This should be a welcomed change, at least from society's perspective. Watching recent documentaries about what is going on behind the scenes in corporate America has left me beyond shocked and saddened. So to know that nothing will be hidden gives me—as well as many others, I'm sure—feelings of great peace. I do think it's hard to accept that on a personal level, that all will be transparent. We hold tight to our secrets."

When you live from your ego, there may be plenty one wishes to hide. When you live from your heart, though, there is nothing to hide. Many of you are already experiencing this. Your secrets are no longer secrets because they no longer matter to you. Truth is what matters. Is that not a relief? As you connect to your hearts, you will find great strength in your ability to be genuine and honest.

"I already feel quite transparent, like an open book. However, there are still things that I wish to keep to myself."

Time will allow you to release any attachments you have. In the higher realms, there is no judgment. All is accepted and respected. Higher vibrational beings don't care if you are heavy in weight, which is your greatest shame. They don't care what you look like. They see your heart. Your heart is your expression of who you are.

"Of course, you touched on the aspect of myself that I have most difficulty accepting."

You have felt judged by others in your life, strangers at the store, many who you come into contact with. If you didn't feel that judgment, you would not find your weight as much of an issue. The judgment makes you feel lesser

185

than and keeps you weighted down.

The fact is your body has protected you from all the changes you are enduring. The extra weight has kept you "safe" and together for this shift. When you see your weight from our prospective, you would not condemn yourself for it. The weight has served its purpose and will soon fall off.

"You've told me that before. And it is so hard to believe because it has felt near impossible to shed any significant amount of weight."

Things are going to change for you very soon. They will change for scores of people as well, even those who have had this issue for most or all of their lives.

"This weight literally weighs me down in all ways. However, you're saying this will change."

You will be well pleased. You will be well pleased for others. You feel the pain of others who are in your shoes, but one day, there will be no pain to feel. Think of it as a gift from Heaven.

"This will be a most appreciated gift. I cannot imagine all the ways this will positively affect all of us who have weight issues."

There will be many other gifts such as these. Life won't be a struggle anymore. Life is meant to be joyful, and it will be joyful. Connect with your heart in any moment and feel the joy. That joy will be a constant in your lives in the new energy. Reaffirm your faith in yourself and who you really are. Tap the deepest and most treasured aspects of you. There you will find joy.

"Many of us will have a hard time believing the part about weight loss. Even for those who have little weight to lose; thoughts about our weight and desired weight loss can consume our minds."

Well, it's time to free your minds. Free your minds of all the heaviness that weighs you down. The thoughts weigh you down more than your weight. Your thoughts about it keep many of you heavy. So imagine freeing the weight from your mind, as much as from your body.

Never before has humankind experienced such difficulty with weight. This has occurred for many reasons. The important thing to do is to start now, today, freeing your mind of the negative self-thoughts you hold. If weight is one of them, start by reversing those thoughts into positive thoughts. Whatever mental chatter that no longer serves who you really are, reverse those thoughts as well.

People hold many negative self-thoughts that run them day after day. Be conscious of this restrictive, unsupportive thinking and free your mind. Ask your angels to help clear these for you. Find ways to not only think supportive thoughts, but also perform supportive actions.

If you think you are not good enough, throw yourself into a project that helps others and see what you are capable of. If you think you are not lovable, go within and learn to love who you are, exactly as you are, and start doing loving actions for just you. If you think you are not intelligent or creative, find things to do that will mirror the intelligence and creativity that lies within, but negative thoughts have held it captive. Set yourself free.

Do you see that experience is everything? Without the experience, it is hard to know anything. Once you understand that you create your life experience and are not victim to it, you are free and empowered to make the changes you so desire. Learn this now if you have not thus far, and then one day, you will experience the ease of living in a higher dimension, and you will have a grand understanding of where you came from.

"You seem to be saying that although life will improve significantly once we shift, it behooves us to understand how our thoughts drive us while we are still in the lower vibrations, that this adds to our growth."

Yes, it behooves you to have this understanding. You're a spiritual being in a physical body and your understanding, your growth is something that you take with you. It completes the human experience. Your soul holds these memories and achievements. They are most desirable.

What also adds to your growth is your ability to "clean up" your life, consciously, and to turn your challenges into successes. When you allow life to mirror what you need to change or heal about yourself, and you honor this gift by responding with new choices, new reactions, or new ways of being—you grow exponentially. You have the choice to ignore the mirrors, but we have already discussed what happens when you do so.

Some of what is coming through to these very pages may be repetitive, but I tell you that the repetition is intentional for those very important points presented here. Your life holds many habits, things you do repetitively, because that is what you grew used to. It may take repeating points in different ways to help you release unsupportive habits.

"Certainly many readers, including myself, need and appreciate the repetition of your points, and in different ways to develop a thorough understanding. Simply speaking, the earth is cleansing herself and we each need to do the same."

That is exactly true. The cleansing of the self may occur without conscious understanding of what is actually occurring from a higher perspective. This is one path, but it is not the easiest one. The easiest path is one where the person is consciously aware of why they are being challenged to choose again, react in a new way, and release the negative parts of self.

"I just had a funny synchronicity. An email came in as

I was writing just now and I tried to ignore it, but felt drawn to open it. This email was selling a product for cleansing and detoxification. Never will I tire of the endless ways that you, the angels, and the Universe validate the messages! Anyways, what I was about to say is that my choice is to always seek ease and effortlessness, although sometimes it is absolutely, downright difficult."

There are some lessons more difficult than others too. You are embarking on your most critical lessons in recent months. Stay strong, and you know to call on us for guidance.

"I have to say that there are times I do call, but although I know my angels are always hearing me, it almost seems as if they are not. Sometimes, it feels as if my angels take a day off. We already touched on this earlier, but is it true that it may feel this way because there are certain things angels cannot interfere with?"

That is an important question and one that many others have. You know that we hear all, and we are always there for each of you. However, there are times we cannot interfere in order to allow you to make the appropriate choice and choose the appropriate reaction, so that you can move on from that lesson. What you may not always see is that we are nudging you and guiding you, yet although you are very aware, you don't see everything that is being presented to you. We can give you all the clues and all the understandings, but you have to act on it. When you act appropriately, you know that you did. This is very empowering. We want you to have that feeling.

"It is empowering, and I relish that feeling when I feel like I finally 'get it.' My frustrations, and even anger, over any given challenging situation can turn into feelings of gratitude and, ultimately, love. My goal is to always look at things from a higher perspective so that I don't react with the frustration and anger. I know that watching our reactions, as well as our thoughts, is absolutely key."

Dig a little deeper and you will find even more wisdom and understanding that helps you through your challenges. You may recognize the person who is challenging you as a member of your soul family who contracted with you prior to your incarnations to teach you this very lesson. Or you find that this was not only a lesson to be learned in this lifetime, but it has been begging to be learned by your soul over several lifetimes. When the lesson is finally learned after lifetimes, there is cause for great celebration.

Your lesson to delve into your self-worth and claim it is not a new one. You have succumbed to this issue in many lifetimes, due to being surrounded by tyrant type personalities again and again. You had to learn to stand up for yourself and acknowledge who you are.

"It makes sense, then, why I used to wear a back brace as a child. I had issues with my 'spine.' It was a physical manifestation of what my beliefs were about myself. And I had back issues again in my adult life until recent years. It seemed that once I started to grow my self-worth, my back issues miraculously resolved themselves."

When you are aware of these physical manifestations, you can better work to resolve issues. There were times you could not stand up straight, and now you never have those issues. As you release parts of you that no longer serve you, your health will improve exponentially. Watch for a shift in health as you release and then raise your vibrations.

"There is so much out there in the media emphasizing disease and dangerous pharmaceuticals, and we are being bombarded with negative messages. You can barely watch a television show without several pharmaceutical ads running throughout it. As I mentioned in my first book, I call this 'fear pollution,' and I feel that these constant, repetitive messages are not good for our health!"

They are not healthy to watch. They can lead to fearful thoughts or have unknown subconscious effects on the self when repeated as they are. These won't be an issue for too much longer. For now, just ignore these messages. Your body, mind, and spirit should concentrate on the positive and creating good health.

In the Golden Age, your health issues will wane, as your bodies are able to allow more light within. Light will heal, as it has healed many of you, but your physical bodies must be able to hold this Light. This is why I say there will be a shift in health as you raise your vibration.

"It is hard for me to put all this information out there that is so incredible, and, yet, what if I'm receiving incorrectly? What if this is my imagination?"

We will not allow that to happen, and your commitment to truth is too strong to allow that to occur. You agreed to this challenge knowing that you would be putting new information out into the world. You feel you are not the likely choice to be doing this; that there are channelers who do readings for others on a daily basis and have much more experience than you, and that makes you second guess yourself.

To quote one of your favorite phrases, "The proof is in the pudding." You have had countless validations that you are receiving correct information, but you still hold some fear. You need to release that now. When this book gets out there, you will see how these messages resonate with many, and then you will see that you were indeed hearing me correctly. You have always wanted to hear my voice with sound, instead of in a telepathic manner. That day will come. Until then, it is your test to trust in your abilities.

Mary, I just asked you to look up the word "gold," as you used to sometimes struggle as to what words are best to describe this new age.

"In the 'Dictionary' application on my Mac computer, one of the definitions of gold that resonated best was: 'a thing that is precious, beautiful, or brilliant.'"

As indeed this new age shall be.

"Golden Age. Just hearing these words makes me feel so full, so excited about our new beginnings. There are times when this shifting is so difficult and challenging; and that is what I'm feeling right now. I feel I have no control over my emotions and state of mind sometimes. This is what I desire to focus on now... the Golden Age."

When you go through various shifts, as you are now, you may feel lonely, sad, and even depressed. Know that these feelings are temporary. Trust the process; surrender to it. These are the times many people shut down, and seek to be alone. Yet I tell you these are the times to open up to us. We can help you through. We can send you reminders, and help and comfort you. Know that our ability to help you through is immense. You can better ease through these difficulties when you call us forth.

"Last night, I had terrible dreams. I woke feeling quite awful, emotionally speaking, and just could not control my mood. So after you spoke this last message to me, I called for the help of one thousand angels. I remember hearing author Doreen Virtue refer to calling for a thousand angels when really needing help. Never before have I done this as I don't want to request more help than what I need. I felt so awful that I truly thought it would take a thousand angels to get me out of this state of mind. I can honestly say my mood has shifted. I felt touches by many and a brightness in my heart that I could not connect with earlier this morning. Now, I am thanking the angels for their help, as I feel stronger now and more connected to myself again. Undoubtedly, I went through this so I could share this experience with others."

When you call us, we are there. You may not see us, but we are there for you. Indeed, you needed to experience this for yourself. You were feeling so low, and everything shifted in a moment for you. It inspired you to take a walk and breathe in the energies from the sky and the mountains and the earth. You have made a complete turnaround just because of your single intention.

"What did the angels do to make me feel so much better?"

They beamed love and Light to you. You were drained of energy and it was as if they filled you right back up. Suddenly, you were filled with hope and joy again.

"As soon as I left for the walk, I saw a bright yellow Volkswagen with the bumper sticker, 'Got Hope?' and it really made me happy. Whenever I see bright yellow anything, I feel it represents a burst of spiritual sunshine."

Colors hold energy just like everything else. You are becoming more aware of the different colors that surround you at different times, knowing that you actually attract different colors to you according to what is going on within you.

"I'm glad I attracted yellow back into my life today. The other thing that happened was that just a couple minutes after I felt the blessing from the angels, I heard loud sirens and a voice being broadcast outside signaling a tornado alarm test. Now that woke me up, and I found the timing so interesting."

You hear sirens, and you automatically feel they are warning you of some difficulty ahead, and often they are. However, the timing of such was in celebration.

"I sit here still in absolute amazement over how much I shifted in just a moment's time. This was an experience I couldn't wait to share with others. When you really need the help, simply ask for it. This tells the Universe that you feel you deserve the help you desire; an intention that is so powerful and rewarding. My gratitude is overflowing."

It is that gratitude that creates an abundance of miraculous occurrences in your life. Feeling gratitude is like bathing whatever your gift is in so much love that it cannot help but attract more of the same. Gratitude is your intense focus of positive energy on something. Like attracts like, and it creates a continuous pattern of receiving gift upon gift.

The angels that blessed you are in celebration that you "got it," that you experienced their combined gifts, took notice of what actually occurred, and are immediately sharing your experience. As excited as you presently are, you are unaware of the true magnitude of your discovery. This will help others in seen and unseen ways, and the impact of this learning experience for you will ripple outward with unexpected effects.

Let me tell you something about your angelic help. Nothing is ever expected in return. They give and give and never expect anything back. Yes, that is unconditional giving and that is what you are all learning to do, too. Just give without expectation. When you give without expecta-tion, you open up those clamps that are metaphorically placed on your hearts. They spring wide open when you allow yourself the freedom to give only for the sake of helping others.

Do you remember when you were a little girl, and you could not understand why people would give so hesitantly, why it often didn't seem natural to them? It is a learned behavior in the third dimensional world because that is what happens when hearts close. There is an expectation that grows, and that need must be fulfilled. There must be a return. But this is also slowly changing. As you grow in

vibration, you grow in your ability to give without expect-
ation.

"That is beautiful and makes so much sense to me. I think there are many of us who give and give and, yet, get so little in return. We may then feel taken for granted."

And those events can end up closing the heart against one's true wishes; it is a protective mechanism. Your intent-ions can help change it so that you no longer attract people who take advantage of you. This does not mean that you go help others by putting them first before you, or do everything for free when you must make a living. It means you take care of yourself first, and help others in the process as long as you stay true to your needs and don't allow the giving to create great conflict for self or another.

Can you accept the changes that are occurring within your heart? Many will feel exposed and vulnerable, but I tell you that as you open your hearts, you will have a strength that you have never been able to count on. You will see things so clearly that there won't be so much doubt and frustration in your life. You will accept things as they occur, and you will willingly recreate your life so that it matches your heart's needs and desires.

"Sometimes, it's hard to know what we truly want in our lives."

That is only when you are disconnected from your heart. Don't you see that when you are truly living from your heart, you are tapping into your greatest wisdom and your deepest desires? Your heart holds the key to vital information that has often been lodged so deep inside and is waiting to be set free. When you open your heart, you are free to be who you really are. There is nothing you can ex-perience as a human that is more freeing than that.

"This reminds me of the saying, 'The light shall set you free.' More specifically, the light shining in our hearts shall set us free. I haven't been talking to my heart lately; I got out of the habit. Perhaps, this is why I've been feeling a little lost lately."

You have been feeling lost because you have been focused on things outside of yourself, mostly because life events forced you to. It takes an immediate shift with your intention to get back on track. What does your heart say to you right now?

"It says, 'You are so loved and supported, and you were forgetting this. You went into a coping state and broke loose from your usual ability to connect.' And then, just as you say, I felt the immediate reconnection. This has taught me to stay connected to my heart. I was all over the place trying to make things work and be well, but I lost conscious connection to my heart."

"I then heard a prophetic statement coming from my heart. It said, 'The showers and storms are almost over, and the rainbow is in sight. Keep your sights on the rainbow. Maintain your composure no matter what you are faced with. Create a space for the magic and miracles to shower you instead.' This makes me so happy. It has been such a difficult couple of weeks, as I was so disconnected."

"Now I feel as if I've opened up the floodgates to my heart: 'The time of hiding in your cave is over. You must open yourself to all the possibilities of spreading your message. You haven't even begun. The opportunities will grow by leaps and bounds. You shall soon see. You will be surprised by the effortlessness as everything will soon come into play. No more holding back; no more room for questioning of the self and what you are capable of. It is time to really get out there.'"

"Okay, that was pretty overwhelming. Now my heart says: 'Can you imagine what your future holds? Think out of the box. From now on *only* think out of the box.'"

You have been so drawn to that statement lately, "to think out of the box." That is because you know that you must heed that directive. This is how many people achieve greatness, to look outside of the normality and the confines they place themselves in. I told you before that you need to release the confines. Not only think out of the box, but also break out of the box you have yourself in.

"I really do get that. Like never before, I realize that I must walk my talk and watch my thoughts closely. Something has truly shifted in me. I understand that my experiences are meant to be shared in this book so that they may inspire others to set themselves free and break away from the third dimensional confines they find themselves in, as well. I am literally visualizing myself busting out of this box that can no longer confine or define me. I feel reborn."

When you release yourself from your old restrictions, you must be vigilant of your thoughts, making sure they are supportive of your new paradigm. Be aware of the little ways those thoughts can return, often through communication with others. You may be fine on your own, with your own thoughts on your own, but when gathered with others, their judgments or different ideas can sabotage your new direction if you allow it to. Always be aware of the company you share things with. A jealous person, for instance, will not serve your own growth.

"We cannot always know who are the best people to share things with."

As your intuition builds, and you are in tuned with your heart, yes, you will be drawn to those who will benefit you, not tear you down. You will be drawn to those who will support you, and not go behind your back. Always intend to surround yourself with like-mindedness so that you have the support that helps you through your growth and as you traverse into new horizons. As you all grow your connections to your hearts, these concerns will increasingly lessen.

"Just recently, I went through another period of time where I was feeling extremely disconnected, even experiencing feelings of worthlessness. I didn't know what to do with myself, and calling a thousand angels for help this time did not work."

Even while you were going through this, you knew that it is during such times that you are preparing for a leap in growth. You didn't know what to do with yourself; you couldn't even write, even though you had been writing every single day. You just wanted to curl up in bed, as you were incubating this transformation that is before you. Yes, as a caterpillar forms into a cocoon, you wanted to just be still, and now you are forming wings and about to fly.

Many of you understand exactly what this process feels like. You have gone through it perhaps more than once, but each time it seems more pronounced and challenging. If so, know that these feelings and experiences, just as for Mary, are only temporary, and you will burst into a new awareness and way of being. It is something that deserves great celebration.

"When going through this process it was especially difficult to control my thoughts."

Life is changing so fast now, that it becomes increasingly important that you let go of old desires, old needs, and old wants. Reassess what you choose for your life in this moment. Desires, needs, and wants can truly become like habits that sometimes need to be broken. In this moment, what is it that you truly desire?

What lines up with your highest vision of yourself? What can you do right now to create this reality? What can you request that with your full faith will manifest into your life? When you tune into your heart, you can answer these questions. Have a conversation with your heart for the purpose of recreating your reality.

Once again, you are at a crossroads, Mary. Do you push your way through or do you allow your way to appear before you? You are making the right choice, and you are not fighting it. Your hurt knee is teaching you to listen within, and listen to you first. You have all the answers you possibly need, so listen now. Listen to your strength and inner knowing. Listen to the gems of information that have been waiting to make themselves known.

When you have a conversation with your heart, there is no room for negative interference you may get in a conversation with a fellow human. There is no jealousy, ulterior motive, half-listening from the heart. It is full on communication with who you really are. What better conversation can you have, Mary? I want you to now have a conversation with your heart, and type the words as you speak.

"I'm sorry I have not listened to you as much as I should have."

Heart: *Regrets are not necessary and only slow you down.*

"What is it you most wish to tell me now?"

Heart: *You are on a fast track to a new life. This life is nothing like what you have been used to. Throw out all expectations so that you don't slow or lessen the new creation you are embarking on. It will seem effortless when you really let go. Keep talking to me and I will guide you every step of the way. There is no way you can go wrong unless you ignore this guidance. All will be more than well.*

"How do I keep an open and constant communication with you?"

199

Heart: *How do you keep an open and constant communication with your family members or friends? I am no different. Think of it as you talking to you. Make talking to you a priority; always put this communication first. You will not be disappointed for I always listen and always have an answer. You can always count on that.*

"It seems I am always talking to you, but it has been unconscious. Now I want to consciously make it a practice. I ask you, how can I get through my fears of putting this book out into the world?"

Heart: *The reason you have been dealing with some fears is because you lost touch with your relentless faith. When you realign with your faith, you will see that you cannot put anything out there that isn't in the highest interest of all who will read this book. Everyone has their own responsibility regarding how they interpret the words and use them in guiding their way through these challenging times. You just concentrate on providing the information, and allow everyone else to respond as they may.*

"Can you give me a guideline regarding how this book will get out there?"

Heart: *It will get out there because this is a most destined project that must get out into the world. You have little reservation in knowing this information is greatly needed out there. You only have your own worries about providing the most accurate information possible. And I tell you again; we will not allow improper information to be released. You are being guided constantly. Everything is going perfectly according to plan. Your relentless faith always, always ends up "kicking in."*

"Yes, 'relentless faith' is one of my favorite phrases, especially with regard to my commitment to following my guidance. I haven't really used this phrase in my writings until this book, but it seems that this is what this book is really about—having relentless faith. With relentless faith, we will succeed in meeting humankind's greatest challenge ever. No matter how difficult it is, no matter how tired we are, no matter how confusing things may be; we must never release the ties we have to our faith in this world's grandest achievement."

"Michael, what else do you want to tell me about communication with the heart?"

What may seem like a small and quiet voice will become louder with practice. And as you consciously communicate with your heart, you'll not only be consciously sparking the connection, but it will also be your heart that will do the "knocking" and will initiate the conversation. When you stray from your path, and once this communication is unlocked, your heart will show you the way.

"Sometimes, I get so confused as to whether something is coming from the Universe itself, the angels, or my own spirit. But then, I realize that it really does not matter. As long as it serves my highest good, and it is coming only from the highest vibrations, I do not really need to know."

When your intentions are set to tap only from the highest vibrations, you can rest assured that the information itself is also from the highest vibrations. You can find comfort in that awareness. Sometimes, it is a combination of sources, all pointing you to a particular understanding.

Imagine what life would be like if everyone were following their inner guidance and the signs of the Universe. One day they will. Until then, you can each be the example. When someone asks why you made that unexpected decision, move, or change, you can tell him or her, "I felt guided to because this is what happened...". That may open up the possibility in another.

Most people are very attached to being in thinking mode; they have no idea that they can be in receiving mode. They do not always have to figure everything out, and they probably are not seeing the whole picture from their thinking part of them. When they open up to guidance, and especially when they open up their hearts, they can make the switch from thinking to receiving. Being in receiving mode opens up a whole new set of possibilities in every aspect of your life.

"I have absolutely no desire to go back to the old ways of going it alone."

And why would you or anyone else who knows what gifts are available to them in every moment? You may be mocked or teased about your way of being, but that is because people make inaccurate judgments about it. Imagine that more and more people are opening up to this new way of being because this will occur. There will be a new paradigm that will be embraced. And many will wonder how they ever coped going it all alone.

As you each open up to these gifts, you will know what true peace is. You have not been able to find peace from outside of you too easily. Perhaps when walking in nature, or when with someone you feel comfortable with or close to. But the kind of peace found through the connection to your soul is unlike the level of peace found in the material world. It is love manifested in you. It is light shining through you. It is finding out who you really are that will bring you your greatest peace.

Why is this so? Because you will understand that you truly are an eternal being that is truly connected to God. You always have and will always be. You are loved by and connected to a Source you have not begun to comprehend. When you feel that connection, you will know peace.

"Many of us know this, on an intellectual level, but

perhaps we have not been capable of truly feeling this."

Feelings are what will help you soar into the Golden Age. Not your thoughts, but your feelings first. This is why I have stated in so many ways that your heart will lead the way. Therefore, it benefits you to start growing your relationship to your heart.

"I really do want to build this relationship. Can you give any other suggestions on how to make this switch to becoming more heart-centered?"

There is a simple way of training yourself to go to the heart. Whenever a situation arises that creates confusion, upset, or mere indecision, place your hand on your heart. This will help you focus your attention there. And then simply tune in and start a conversation. Allow your heart to lead you. Begin giving your heart the permission to be leader, and see what happens.

"As I tried this just now, I found it so helpful to have a tactile reminder. I feel such a peaceful presence within my heart, and it actually calms me down."

Once you accept this new way of being, it will come naturally, without making the conscious redirection. You will naturally connect with your heart just as you now naturally call on a loved one or friend for help or advice. You find that you, yourself, provide an invaluable resource in all situations that arise. You learn to trust and respond with full conviction and determination.

"I've made several decisions this morning by allowing my heart to lead. Truly, my mind did not agree, but I trusted my heart. My mind went into fear, and my heart then calmed me."

That is the peace I am talking about. Always tune in to connect with that peace no matter what is going on outside of you. Think of your heart as your retreat.

"We all need a retreat with all these difficulties

surrounding us. We can retreat into love."

Love will never disappoint you. That you can trust. Love always wins in the end. Retreat into love and you will endure always. You will have all the tools you need to make this transition into the Golden Age. There is another one we haven't yet discussed.

"What is it?"

Laughter. When you laugh, you raise your vibration. Keep your sense of humor always, and you will ride the waves much easier. Laugh to yourself, and especially laugh with others, as it is a contagious act. We laugh all the time in the higher realms. We feel your joy when you laugh. Your laughter actually brings more Light within... so laugh.

"When I get into fits of uncontrollable laughter, those are some of my happiest times although I feel I can barely physically endure it when it is really out of control. When that happens though, I do feel a release. It feels as if my troubles melt away, but I never thought of it as a time when we receive more Light."

Of course, in that same vein, your smiles also bring more light. This should not surprise you. Anything positive and happy brings light, and that which is negative and sad puts a veil on the light.

"Author Sherri Cortland says that a simple smile can raise one's vibration better than anything else. I had never really thought of it in that particular way, but it makes sense, as does with laughter."

Make no mistake that you are constantly vibrating at differing levels of light. There is no stagnant measurement, as it is constantly fluctuating. This is why, at any moment, you can make a new choice and shift your vibration. Change your perspective on things and watch your vibration change. See the humor even when you're going through a difficult time, and shift the vibration of it.

"That is what I recently experienced when I badly sprained my knee. It made me extremely immobile, but there was much humor to be had. Such as when I was ever so slowly walking with crutches and met the slightest incline on a sidewalk, I would say, 'Big hill!' I don't think I've ever laughed so much during a trying time. Perhaps this was one of the reasons I experienced the injury."

That is a very high way of looking at things. Your injury did happen for many reasons, as you know.

Try something. Whisper to yourself in your mind the words, "I Am Love." Now in your mind, shout the words, "I Am Love," and with feeling. Do you feel the difference?

"When I whispered, I felt something. But when I shouted it loudly in my mind, I *really* felt something. I could almost feel my cells rejoicing. I know that sounds funny, but that is just what it felt like; it was as if it caused great movement of my cells, and energy just flowing through my body. How amazing that it is being felt so powerfully."

Your cells respond to love—the feeling of love. When you say, "I Am Love," your cells experience the feeling of love, and this is positive energy being moved throughout your cells and all parts of your body and all levels of your being. If you want to fully heal your sprain, keep telling yourself that you are love! If you want to heal anything, spread the love around.

"I feel like I just took the best supplement I could ever take. My body feels like it is singing now. This is so simple and yet extremely powerful. My mood has brightened even more so. 'I Am Love!' Certainly it is the feelings behind it that are most important, to really feel love."

Work with this.

"Immediately after channeling you now, I listened to

my CD, 'Feeling Joyful & Abundant in a Changing World.' It has been several months since I had listened to it. Someone just ordered a copy, and I felt compelled to listen to it again. It's an interactive CD and at the very end of it, I ask the listener to 'Repeat these most powerful words: I am love, I am love, I am love...'. Truly, I forgot that I ended it that way. Surely, you whispered to me to listen to it, but only after I channeled this message."

You are perfectly correct. You were putting that out there, but were not saying the words to yourself. Just keep saying these words now.

"Once again, I need to walk my talk."

Heaven waits as you find the love in each of you. Find the love and feel it into every part of your being. This exercise will allow you to feel immediate results. You find just how powerful you are, and how powerful your feelings are. When you become love, the old parts of you fall away. The regrets, the grief, the hurt, the pain; they flow out as you grow the love within.

Who hurt you today, yesterday, last week, or ten years ago—and you're still feeling the pain? Feel that right now. Feel it in your heart. Now tell your heart with great feeling, "I Am Love." What happened to the hurt? Does love forgive it? If not, tell it again and again until you fill up with so much love you cannot possibly hold the hurt any longer. Choose to be love and hold onto love always. Love will free you from your pain. Love will move you to your highest expression of self.

"There are people in my life who are beautiful examples of being great expressions of love, and I naturally gravitate toward them. My dear friend, Clare, has said for years that she is ultimately here to just 'be love.' I really understand what she means now; she has always known this. I see how we can help each other to be love by being examples; constantly putting out these positive vibes, positive energies, as they are so powerful and contagious."

Love is contagious! That pull is coming from your own heart to nurture the positive acts of others and be in that place with them. You start with yourself; then like attracts like, and you find yourself elevated to a higher place. Embrace the contagion. Your heart will always guide you. Celebrate and appreciate the growing love on your planet.

"How do we help our children incorporate the teachings in this book into their lives?"

The youth of this world will shift much easier than those who are older in age. They have incarnated with gifts that allow them to ease into the transition much more smoothly. They haven't been on this earth as long, have not developed the fears and misbeliefs their parents may have developed, and don't have so much of the "old" to shed. All these same principles can be taught to the youth, primarily by example and whatever is age appropriate. Teach your children to be love. That is the most important quality you can instill in your child.

"For years, I have wanted to write a book about raising spiritually aware children. It is especially difficult for children to tap into their spiritual selves when society does not nurture or support this. But once we shift, we will all be fully aware, correct?"

The path of learning and growing is never complete. It will always continue on. This is why many teachers say to concentrate on the journey, not the destination. The journey never ends, so be in the moment—be in it.

Look around you now. Can you imagine life any different than it is now? Can you imagine how people will sustain their mental and emotional acuities when the shift occurs? It all seems so foreign and abrupt. Yet to us, it is the most natural progression you can make. It is anything but abrupt, as it has been in the making for eons of time. Discover the joy of the most exciting process a soul has ever journeyed. You are all going through it together, and together you will create Heaven on earth. Summon all the tools and invisible helpers that will lead you to this new destination. And allow Heaven to shower you with a new life beyond your imaginings.

CHAPTER 6

A Fifth Dimensional Miracle

*C*an you allow for a miracle in your life? A miracle that will create the most beautiful feelings you have ever experienced? Then, I ask you now to call on love. Call on love, right now. Literally say, "I Call on Love." Does this seem silly to you? I promise you it is not, for these are very powerful words. When you "Call on Love," you are calling forth a miracle in your life. It is a call to your angels and the Universe to bring love forth in some way. Just give it a try.

"I called on love and then went into meditation. Immediately, I saw a circle shape in my third eye starting large and then becoming increasingly smaller as it moved away from me. I see that often. What is that?"

That is your I Am presence, your soul presence in connection with you.

"As I was seeing that, in the middle of my vision I saw a boat on water. I kept calling on love. Then I saw an image of an eye. That is something I also continually see in meditation. What do these things mean?"

What do you feel they mean?

"That I am moving toward my I Am presence. I am moving toward who I really am as I sail on the waters of life? I feel that when I 'Call on Love,' the miracles are really going to set sail in my life."

Indeed, you are in fine creation mode. Let this example inspire readers to do the same, to "Call on Love."

And let us now take it a step further. When you are sad—call on love. When you are troubled—call on love. When you are tired and weak—call on love. Instead of voicing a complaint, simply say—"I Call on Love."

This will attract the forces of the Universe to bring you to a state of pure love, which is what you really are. When you are love, you cannot possibly be sad, lonely, angry, depressed, upset, or hopeless. Call on who you really are. Allow the Universe to help bring you to yourself. And just be love.

There will be those who will not bother to speak these words, unaware of the power behind what seem to be mere words. Free will is for all. Those who choose to try a simple, yet powerful exercise can see if this invites miracles into their lives. It is all your free choice.

"How is 'I Call on Love' different from saying 'I Am Love' to the body?"

"I Am Love" is a statement to self of who you really are. This brings your self into perfect alignment to attain its full potential.

When you "Call on Love," you are actively choosing for

universal influences to come into your awareness and make positive change! You are asking for love to show itself, and it will come through in ways that only love can provide. Love breeds miracles and calling on it will bring forth unimaginable synchronicities resulting in the manifestation of a fifth dimensional miracle or an array of miracles. Pure love exists in the fifth dimension. Concentrate on love and find yourself on the path to your destined new home.

(the next day)

"Today in meditation, I just knew that this time I would see a vision of a sunrise and then I immediately saw a sunrise in my third eye. It went away and then came back again. Was this prophetic on my part, or am I actually creating my third-eye visions?"

You are creating your visions and if you could only understand the power of that.

"Did you whisper to me to think of a sunrise, and to expect an image of a sunrise to prove this point?"

Yes, we did whisper to you, and you heard and acted and realize now that you can create these visions.

So when you "Call on Love," can you imagine what you are creating? You have no idea of what you set into motion yesterday when you spoke these words.

"Explain what you mean, 'If you could only understand the power of that.'"

You created a vision from the all-knowing part of you. The more you get in touch with that, the easier you will manifest anything you desire. Use this as another tool to connect with the power of you. When I speak to Mary, I am speaking to all of you. Mary knows that throughout this book and journey she is an example so she can share what she experiences to help you understand what I am teaching. When I speak to her, I am really speaking to all of you

211

who wish to listen.

You may say that you have never seen a vision in your third eye before. But I ask you, have you tried? Years ago, it took Mary nearly an hour of being in meditation before she could see an image, and now it takes a very brief period of time. As you shift and raise your vibrations, all these tools are easier to connect with. Some of you see visions in your fully conscious self and don't need to go into meditation. This is where you are all heading, where you will see interdimensionally.

"We are already getting glimpses of this. So many of us are seeing little white or colored sparks of energy. And now our photographs are showing us orbs. I cannot doubt that we are moving toward seeing interdimensionally. Is there anything we can do to improve our abilities to really see?"

As always, intention is the most powerful creator of new opportunities and abilities. When you are busy with living, it may be difficult to see what you are actually capable of seeing. Therefore, you can take periods of time to actually ask yourself what you see. Next time you are looking at someone, ask yourself, for instance, if you see his or her aura. Or when you go outside in your garden, can you see the energies around your plants? Do an open-eyed meditation where you sit in a dimly lit room with your eyes open, quiet the mind, and see what happens.

"I love that idea of an open-eyed meditation and will try this."

Weeks later, since I began to "Call on Love," I had the privilege of seeing Braco, (pronounced "Brahtzo") the Croatian healer, in Sedona and San Francisco (www.bracoamerica.com). Through his healing gaze at hundreds of people at a time gathered in a room, miracles occur, sometimes spontaneously. They are thrilling to witness. I felt such love coming from this man, and felt that the energy he was channeling was a preview of what we all will experience one day. He is giving us a taste of the new energy!

You gathered your family, and against common sense that told you that kind of money should not be spent, you took them on these trips to see him and that intention has resulted in the creation of a new life for all three of you. The fact is that it set something in motion that you are still not aware of.

"When will I become aware?"

Your desire to understand what is yet to be unveiled does not go unnoticed, but you are not quite ready for this unveiling. There is such a thing as too much information too soon. But continue to expect the unexpected in a most glorious way.

"I'm overjoyed to hear that. Regarding your suggestion about practicing open-eyed meditation, gazing with Braco felt like an open-eyed meditation. Although I don't regularly see people's auras, I saw his aura during each session that he gazed at us. The interesting thing was that as I saw his aura, I began seeing the auras of others in the room."

Let that give you an idea of how love shows itself. The room was filled with love, which brought up everyone's own vibration, which in turn allowed you to see a physical representation of that.

"I'll never forget what that felt like. It made me feel very excited about our future, when love is the way."

Do you know what happens when you receive a

miracle? We in the Heavenly realms celebrate. We celebrate your being touched by God's gifts. At the moment you experience the gift, we feel what you feel, and it is a gift for us, as well. We delight in your delight. We know what is about to occur and we often give you signs that a miracle is on its way. Have you noticed?

"Absolutely. I know when something good is coming. It makes it even more exciting because there is anticipation, even though the specifics may not be consciously known. The most miraculous experiences in my own life were not even perceived by my own imagination. That is what makes them especially grand."

People may not consider what I'm about to describe as a miracle as far as synchronicity is concerned, but to me it is. Prior to this book going into publication, I had a bit of a disaster occur at our house. The robotic arm of a garbage truck pulled down the phone, cable, and electrical wires, which brought down the telephone pole at the corner of our lot, and all that goes with it, right onto our property and adjoining properties. No one was hurt, thankfully. I initially felt that this symbolized that things are "falling," and yet we will be just fine. Just a few days after that, they removed our road and replaced it with new asphalt. Just a few months following that, a new home was moved onto a new foundation built right across the street from our house.

After the electric company replaced the pole and adjoining wires, and I hired an electrician to replace the electrical panel and wiring attached to the house, we had all new wiring and new components, which I sensed symbolized "new energy."

After our road was repaved, I felt that literally symbolized a "new road." The new house that was moved onto a brand new foundation across the street symbolized a "new home." It seems to me that these events miraculously occurring so beautifully close together, validated the new energy, new road, and, ultimately, our new home in the Golden Age that has been described throughout this book.

CHAPTER 7

Stairway to the Golden Age

There are seven steps described by Archangel Michael below that will help lead you on your path to creating Heaven on earth. All of these have been described in detail throughout this book. As you will see, with each step, it is all about living from the inside out.

The Seven Golden Steps:

One. *Choose love over fear*
Two. *Lead from your heart*
Three. *Clear away the old*
Four. *Love and forgive without condition*
Five. *Embrace change*

Six.   *Connect with angels and signs*
Seven.   *Allow the Light*

Golden Step One: Choose love over fear

What were the thoughts you woke up with this morning? Were they thoughts of gratitude and love, or of worry and fear? Make it a practice to start your day stating what you are grateful for, or just making a simple and yet profound statement of gratitude such as, "I am deeply grateful for all that I am." Feel love in your heart and let it pervade your whole being.

Show loving kindness to yourself when you look in the mirror, when you make a mistake, or when you slip into a fear-based thought. Let love wash over you, as it cleanses and heals. When you're at the grocery store, show loving kindness to others. Smile and send love from your heart. When you're driving on the road and someone cuts you off, realize that you have done the same before, intentionally or not, and stay in that state of love. Do not let others deter you from feeling love and expressing loving kindness. Do not judge others. You have no idea what their experiences are and what they are going through.

When you find yourself in a situation that brings on fear-based thoughts, ask your angels to help you through it. Ask them to help you see things clearly and look for signs from the Universe—synchronicities—which provide guidance as well. When you change your mindset from one based in fear to one based in love, you may sometimes revert back to your old ways of thinking and feeling. Merely choose a new thought and accept that you will have setbacks, but your intention to choose love over fear is what will create just that. Maintain the intention.

Golden Step Two: Lead from your heart

Stop listening to society, the news, the forced ideas on you of what's right and what's wrong, and start listening to your heart. Connect with your soul and start or continue leading through your feelings, your gut, your knowingness. There are so many ways to do this. The simplest way to begin is to just talk to your heart and then listen. Your heart is speaking to you all the time. Are you listening?

Your heart holds such wisdom. It knows all, but you were not trained and brought up to think and be this way. Yes, of course, you work with your mind as well, but you lead with your heart in conjunction with all other supportive elements in your new way of being. Your heart knows the way to creating Heaven on earth. Just listen and be guided. Work together and soon you will work as one. You will mesh with your soul, you with you, and become who you really are.

Golden Step Three: Clear away the old

It is time to embrace all the lessons that are right before you now. This is of great significance. If you keep experiencing the same trials again and again, recognize and understand the lesson behind it. Be aware, monitor your reactions, and make new choices so that you can move on from these lessons. Clear out the rage, regrets, bitterness, and such, and replace those feelings for positive ones. Release the past! Make peace with yourself, knowing that you came on this earth to move through these lessons, and celebrate yourself for your every success. All of your lessons, at their very core, are lessons of unconditional love and forgiveness.

What are you attached to that no longer serves you? Is

219

it your need to call a friend the moment you're confronted with something difficult, before you've even allowed yourself time to process and explore it? Is it your habit of wasting time on things you know don't serve you, but are just used to? Are you attached to your dramas and difficulties and don't want to let them go? Are you attached to people who don't support your growth and rather tend to stagnate you? Consider what attachments no longer serve you and release them.

Yes, of course I'm talking about material things, possessions, as well. As you become more enlightened, many of these items lose their meaning or are no longer desirable. Release these too. Reduce the clutter and try to maintain as much simplicity and order as possible, as they are a reflection of what is going on in your mind. As you clear your mind, you clear your outside surroundings, and it works the other way, as well. Simplify all aspects of your life, and it will rejuvenate you.

Golden Step Four: Love and forgive without condition

Who do you still need to forgive? Make a mental list and start forgiving! You may be on this list, as the self often is. Provide yourself the freedom you desire deep down and forgive. Let go and feel the joy and freedom in your heart as you cut the connections and ties that do not serve you.

Every enemy, every hurtful thing another has done to you, has led to your spiritual growth. This is why you are here—to grow—and they have helped you accomplish this growth. However, this does not mean you must go to that person, personally forgive them, and possibly succumb to more hurt or difficulty. It can also be a silent letting go, a releasing of your attachment to anger, and a knowing that once the lesson is learned, you can move forward. You cannot move forward, however, without providing forgiveness. So forgive and let go. Let go and let God.

Forgiveness yields freedom of the heart. When you hold anger and grudges toward others, your heart cannot express that which it is. Love is held inside waiting to be released, not just to you and others in your life, but to the world and everything in it. Your heart desires to be open, not bound up tight and closed off. So forgive, and transmute those negative feelings into love. Love heals all things.

As you allow yourself to forgive, you allow yourself to fully be one who loves. You can just be love no matter what. Forgiveness frees your heart to be love, as love is the new way.

Golden Step Five: Embrace change

It is inherent in most of you to resist change. The act of embracing change may seem to be one of your greatest challenges. When you realize that you chose this time to be on earth to experience and help bring forward the greatest change this earth has ever experienced, and the Universe has ever seen, you also realize you signed up to embrace change.

You can resist it and make it much harder for yourself—or begin to experience new things and understand the new way. Is it not better to feel the ecstasy of Heaven within you than to not feel it? Is it not better to work with the angels and receive their help than go it alone? Is it not better to release negative thinking and manifest what you desire than be held victim to your fear-filled thoughts and creations? Is it not better to attract new friends and soul family that support your purpose than hold onto those who stifle it?

Golden Step Six: Connect with angels and signs

When you open your eyes to the gifts of Heaven, as the angelic realms await your permission to let them help you in your life, you will have found your greatest treasure. Your angels will be your best support outside of your true self to help you create Heaven on earth. And it all starts with your desire and permission.

You can develop a direct relationship with Heaven that will grow exponentially. The gifts are endless, and your mind will open to possibilities even beyond your imagination. You will see, hear, feel, and experience magic and miracles that will astound you. You will never be bored with life, and you will never feel alone again. You will feel the love, the bliss, and the ecstasy of Heaven, and it will help you begin your life anew.

Feel the touch of an angel and experience the love they have for you. Notice the constant signs they are showering you with, either directly or through synchronicity. Let them guide you to what is always in your highest interest and see your life explode into glorious opportunities and blessings. And feel gratitude for what all of your angels and all beings in the Heavenly realms do for you.

You know now, if you didn't before, that your angels use glorious synchronicity to give you messages. Be aware of these signs of love and guidance, and, of course, you also attract them from the Universe itself. See the constant mirrors displayed by the Universe to you every day. Those days of wondering and pondering and questioning everything in your life are nearing the end!

Golden Step Seven: Allow the Light

As your vibration rises, you will have the ability to receive more and more of the Light of God. This Liquid Light is what will eventually feed you in all ways. It will allow you to become the Light being you really are as you release all that no longer serves you. You become you, as you become graced with the Light. The Light allows you to reside in this new place called Heaven on earth.

Note: The Seven Golden Steps are explored and studied in greater detail through *Michael's Seven Golden Steps E-Course*. This is an independent course study guided by Archangel Michael and based on his channeled teachings in this book. Find out more about this intensive, life-changing course at www.marysoliel.com.

CHAPTER 8

A Final Word

*Y*ou now have a glimpse into the Golden Age before you. *You also have the tools you need to help prepare you for this most glorious transition that humans have ever experienced. Hug and hold and love each other through this process. Allow the best of yourselves to beam outward at all times. Your destiny is great and your mission is highly challenging. We know what you are going through in every moment and we will help you through. Know that at this time, we see the greater picture and we can guide you. Accept our guidance and our love to help you find your way.*

The glories of the Golden Age will be more wondrous than any one book, or speech, or course can describe. This has given you a small window to your new reality. Fill your hearts with the wonder and imagination of a child, and truly open up to the gifts that will be bestowed upon you. With your hearts opening, this implosion of love will find a new way of being as humans in a very new and grand reality. Deep in your hearts, you know this—all of this—to be true.

Be easy on yourselves and each other. Create a space for forgiveness at all times. Set your heart free and love without condition. This is what being love is. It is a most wondrous way to be. If you find yourself closing your heart and reverting to the "old ways," just speak to your heart and remind yourself that, "I Am Love." This helps you and the world itself.

You are all celebrated as the great pioneers creating this great Golden Age. You each hold the Light, and as your Light grows, you become human Light bearers who raise the vibration of the planet so high that you change it forevermore. This is why you are here. This is what you have worked toward over countless incarnations. The time has come to, ultimately, be Light. I am Archangel Michael.

ABOUT THE AUTHOR

Mary Soliel is an author, visionary, spiritual teacher, and self-described "synchronist." Her three-time award winning book *I Can See Clearly Now: How Synchronicity Illuminates Our Lives* is a groundbreaking exploration of the exciting phenomenon of synchronicity.

As a channel of Archangel Michael, the publishing of this book highlights Mary's new beginning as a teacher and messenger to globally raise awareness of the Golden Age before us. *The New Sun,* which features more life-changing and pioneering inspiration from the Archangel, including wisdom from several guest teachers in the Heavenly realms, is considered to be a sequel to this book. Both *Michael's Clarion Call* and *The New Sun* are award-winning finalists in the 2013 International Book Awards.

Mary is available for U.S. and international speaking engagements and workshops, and radio/print/television interviews. Please visit her at: www.marysoliel.com.

CPSIA information can be obtained
at www.ICGtesting.com
Printed in the USA
LVOW13s2059280218
568203LV00026B/482/P